Should I Leave My Relationship or Not?

Should I Leave *My* Relationship *or* Not?

The Smart Woman's Guide to a Clear Path Forward

KAREN LIN

NEW YORK

LONDON • NASHVILLE • MELBOURNE • VANCOUVER

Should I Leave My Relationship or Not?

The Smart Woman's Guide to a Clear Path Forward

© 2021 Karen Lin

Published in New York, New York, by Morgan James Publishing in partnership with Difference Press. Morgan James is a trademark of Morgan James, LLC. www.MorganJamesPublishing.com

ISBN 9781631951169 paperback
ISBN 9781631951176 eBook
ISBN 9781631951183 audiobook
Library of Congress Control Number: 2020934793

Cover & Interior Design by:
Christopher Kirk
www.GFSstudio.com

Editor:
Emily Tuttle

Book Coaching:
The Author Incubator

Author Photo:
Loan Le Butler

Morgan James is a proud partner of Habitat for Humanity Peninsula and Greater Williamsburg. Partners in building since 2006.

Get involved today! Visit
MorganJamesPublishing.com/giving-back

For Ann, my soul sister.
You're my pillar of unconditional support
and encouragement. We're making
all our dreams come true. Thank you
for agreeing to do all the things with me!

Table of Contents

Foreword

"I just need a clear path forward. Then I'll know..."

It's not every day that I run across a resource that so fully resonates with my intention to live my life at the 'Meta-Level' or higher-level as I have with Karen Lin's beautifully written and engaging debut *Should I Leave My Relationship or Not? The Smart Woman's Guide to a Clear Path Forward.*

Who are our best teachers? Those who have walked in our shoes and stumbled, fallen, and even so, find the tools, resources, strength, and wisdom to make dramatic and massive shifts. A Wise Teacher will then share the wisdom, the *magic elixir,* with others, just like all heroes on a journey do. That is exactly what Karen Lin has done.

Karen provides readers grappling with the question 'should I leave my relationship or not' a process for a clear and loving path forward resulting in clarity and peace.

Karen Lin is a well-respected coach who works with smart and confident women helping them on a journey to discover clarity, freedom, fearlessness, and peace. She now shares her skills as an author in this generous resource designed to help you gain clarity and resonate with your core being as you navigate this big question.

From the book, I must share these highlights:

- The wisdom found on page 26 alone is enough reason to buy and read this book cover to cover. I literally felt my blood flush throughout my body as I resonated with this golden nugget of enlightenment.

- Take advantage of Karen's CLEAR ME process and eliminate confusing emotions and contradictory thoughts as you learn to LEAD with love and engage your body in the decision-making process.

- And, the 'Best-Self Visualization' found in Chapter 4 is nothing short of brilliant.

When Karen asked me to read her manuscript and write this foreword I felt honored and was happy to do so. But then, in the reading, something happened…

It never occurred to me that this amazing book would be a valuable 'pre-assessment' asset. I'm not contemplating leaving a relationship. Instead, I am entering a new relationship, one in which I want to enter from the same place described on page 19, where the power of my most loving, self-activated being shows up and activates the most caring parts and most loving-self of my new love interest. I am looking forward to this new journey empowered with the tools and wisdom found in this lovely book.

Thank you, Karen!

-Sarah Saint-Laurent

Sr. Principal Leadership Consultant and Author

Chapter 1:

Should I Stay or Go?

Megan was about to drift off. Then she heard a whisper, "Please love me. Please love me." She could feel George hovering over her, his warm breath almost a light breeze through her hair. Her eyes were closed, but she could picture him squinting with his brows slightly furrowed. That's the way he looked when he was concentrating intently on the task in front of him. She stayed as relaxed as possible. She didn't want him to know she could hear him—she wished she hadn't. She already felt guilty for wanting to leave him. Deep down, he did know something was wrong. Megan sighed inwardly and fell asleep.

Megan and George Atkins met their senior year in college and got married right after graduating. They had two daughters, Rachel and Cassandra, two years apart, who were both in college now. She thought back to the week before their wedding. Most of the preparations were done and the young couple were about to head to Vegas for the weekend for a family reunion with the rest of the extended Atkins clan. Before they left, Megan pulled her friend Jessica aside. She wrung her hands together as she tried to describe how she felt.

Megan said, "Jessica, I've been thinking. The wedding is almost here. And I just don't feel anything."

She scanned Jessica's face, and Jessica replied, "Well, you've been swamped with wedding preparations. I would be numb too. Aren't you leaving for Vegas tomorrow?"

"That makes sense. Yes, I have to pay Vivian for the floral arrangements. Will you see her later? Maybe I could give you the money instead. That would be such a load off and then I can finish packing."

"Of course. Enjoy the trip and we'll talk when you get back."

Megan mulled over her conversation with Jessica. She didn't seem to be alarmed. Everything was paid for, and tickets for the honeymoon were booked; Megan felt like she was on an unstoppable train. She tossed her brown hair, focused on the task in front of her, and placed her favorite blue shift, perfect for a Vegas buffet, into the open luggage.

Megan and George were the last ones to arrive. The family reunion was actually planned before the wedding date was finalized. They found the perfect wedding venue and the only dates available were July 14, which gave them four months to plan, or June 3 the following year. They settled on July 14. So here they were on July 6 at the Bellagio Hotel and Casino. George's sister Dana ran up with a book and shoved it into Megan's hands before saying hello. "Here, you might want to read this on your honeymoon." Megan looked down. *The History of Worms*.

"Uh, thanks, Dana," Megan said in her bemused state.

Then all the cousins came bounding in. Megan didn't know who was who. George's mom was one of ten kids, so George had twenty cousins. A few of them had just started families, so there were also a couple of babies in the mix. All of George's cousins had the same smart, bookish look. The family joke was that they would buy a family compound so everyone could grow up together. There was an ENT doctor, an eye doctor, a pediatrician, an OB/GYN, a dentist, a lawyer, a mechanical engineer, an electrical engineer, an accountant, a programmer, and a biologist. They had all the makings necessary for a little overeducated family village. The older generation loved this utopian idea and joked that they were looking for some land, but Megan wasn't sure it was a joke. The Atkinses felt warm and familiar compared to her own family. Megan hadn't grown up visiting her relatives much and didn't know her cousins all that well. This was so different.

Megan and George excused themselves so they could finish checking in. They hurried upstairs, left their bags, and rushed back down to meet the crew. Megan was staying in a room with Dana and her mom, and George was staying with his dad. By the time they got back downstairs, all of George's aunts and uncles had arrived. The extended family was almost fifty strong by the time they accounted for everyone. Then they made their way to go see the famous Cirque du Soleil show *O*. Uncle Thomas led the way. "I have your tickets, everybody. Try not to lose me," he shouted.

That night, the "kids" gathered and played mafia. Megan learned that George was the emotional cousin when he stormed out of the room because he felt like there was some unfair collusion happening. The game night wrapped, and everyone went back to their rooms. Megan lay down and picked up a book she brought. It had some tips for intimacy and honeymoon advice. Dana had been watching TV. She glanced over, saw what Megan was reading, and immediately turned off the TV and the lights. Megan stared into the darkness a bit stunned but closed her book and said goodnight. "What a family," she thought. George's family, soon to be her family, quirks and all. She smiled into the pitch blackness, closed her eyes, and quickly drifted off.

Jessica and Megan met up again when she got back from Vegas, the wedding only two days away.

Megan volunteered her thoughts cheerfully, "You know what, Jessica, I've never really had a big warm loving family. I feel like I'm being adopted into this big Greek family, even though no one is Greek, and I feel really good about everything."

Jessica looked visibly relieved and replied, "I'm glad. It sounds like you got what you needed by getting away for a bit."

"I think so, too."

Megan and George got married in a beautiful ceremony surrounded by hundreds of friends and family, in a majestic dusty rose–colored ballroom with matching bridesmaid dresses and hundreds of roses.

The first year together was hard, as they fought and made up repeatedly. But that was normal, Megan told herself. Things got better the second year, and they started a family. Rachel came first and was smart as a whip. She loved to organize and arrange things—stack the magazines on the table, line up the shoes by the door, fold the napkins on the table. Then Cassandra came along, and she liked to undo everything that Rachel started. Some days they were a joy; some days they were a terror to manage. Sometimes, Megan felt trapped. She thought back to the day when she had that conversation with Jessica. What if she had told Jessica how she really felt … that it was cold feet, doubt? But how would she have said it? What reasons did she have?

Megan took on some extra responsibility while George got his PhD, and now he was a professor at the university. George was supportive while Megan attended all the trainings required for her to become the head of her HR department.

One day, when the girls were ten and eight, George was out of town. Megan called the babysitter to come watch the kids, and she checked into a hotel. That nagging feeling that she was in the wrong relationship was back. She thought about her vows, which meant something to her, of course. She decided she just needed to make more time for her own hobbies. She pushed the thoughts away and went out to dinner to try to clear her mind.

Five years passed. Megan and George were in a gorgeous new home: midcentury modern and sleek, with gorgeous light flowing in through the floor-to-ceiling windows. Her friends would come over and their jaws would drop. She designed the closets herself. More than one of her friends had immediately called their husbands over and shouted, "I need one of these ASAP!" When her parents would visit, George would get advice from her dad on the garden. George was great with her parents and never seemed to mind how long they would visit.

Then, after her parents were heading home after the holidays and George had already gone to bed, Megan surveyed the view. Everything felt peaceful and calm as she turned down the light dimmers. When she got upstairs, George was snoring. She held his nose for a few seconds, just long enough for him to stir and stop snoring. She only needed a minute to fall asleep. As she drifted off, she thought, "Should I really leave all this? I have everything. I should be happy."

Five more years went by. Now both girls were in college. Megan and George had accomplished a lot together and were pillars in their community. She was proud of their home. She had her own hobbies. But if she just thought about George, it wasn't a particularly rewarding relationship. Everything was okay. She thought about all that she had to be grateful for. How women all over the world would love to have what she had, would die to be in her shoes. It made her feel awful, ungrateful, and guilty for wanting to leave. She loved George, but she wasn't in love. She wasn't sure she ever had been. She wanted to leave, but how could she leave after all this time?

Megan went to work. Today one of the vendors sent a field rep to give presentations on filling out inspection reports properly. He had worked for and retired from two different cities and now he was working in the private sector. He was older and had decades of experience. He called Megan "darling" and "honey" because that's the era he came from. He wasn't politically correct, but he had a funny story to share every day.

Megan had to ask, "Don, what made you take this job?"

Don replied, "I was retired. I stayed home for one week and then came right back to work. My wife already had a daily routine at home, and I was just getting in the way."

"Do you like to travel?"

"I would like to. But my wife doesn't enjoy it and it would be hard, so I've chosen to work instead."

"Have you thought about doing it on your own?"

"Well, I thought about leaving. But at my age, I can't really afford the alimony. We don't really have any options. And working makes the day go by pretty quick."

Megan was stunned into silence, and Don went on with one of his stories. Another colleague approached just as Don was launching into his Cuban Missile Crisis story. A group was gathering. Don had the whole crew holding their sides laughing hysterically as he regaled everyone with his stories of accidental bravery and stupidity.

That night Megan stared at the ceiling. She thought, "I'm forty-five. Half my life is behind me. Half my life is still ahead of me. I have to make a decision. And if I'm going to leave, I need to decide soon … before I lose my nerve or some weird thing happens like one of us loses our job or gets sick, and then I feel obligated to stay."

The next morning, Megan looked at herself in the mirror. It was the first time she realized she didn't recognize herself anymore. *Who are you?* She thought about Don coming out of retirement to work because he and his wife couldn't spend that much time together. He filled out inspection reports as the better option.

She didn't want to waste the years she had left in ambivalence. It made her feel horrible. "I just need a clear path forward. Then I'll know if I should leave my husband or not."

And that's why Megan needed me. She needed an objective way to figure out her clear path forward. She couldn't talk to any of her friends or family anymore. Megan had so many voices in her head already that she felt like she wasn't even sure what she believed in anymore or if any of those voices were even hers. She wanted a safe place to explore the possibility of leaving without feeling like a horrible person and heretic. She also needed more than just talk; she needed real tools that could help her evaluate what mattered most and how to get behind her own decision.

So, I showed Megan the process I'm going to show you, helped her decide if she should leave her relationship or not. Megan felt like she might break under the constant deluge of doubt, uncertainty, fear, and guilt. Something had to change but she didn't know what more she could do. She hated that she didn't recognize herself anymore and was ready to find the parts of herself that she had lost. Using my process, we addressed the underlying causes of her turmoil to help her feel confident and optimistic about her future. My process gave her a clear and loving path forward that resulted in clarity and peace. And now, I'm going to show this process to you.

Chapter 2:

Good Reasons to Stay

I met Ben right after graduating from college. It was a blind date that a mutual friend from the church we belonged to set us up on. He was Taiwanese; I was Taiwanese. Why not, right? At the time, he was getting his master's degree and working at a nonprofit in Los Angeles. I was just starting my career as a civil engineer in Dallas.

We managed to connect and had our first date at the Cotton Patch. He brought a friend, and I brought a friend. We chatted over chicken-fried steaks the size of his head (and he had a large head!). He was a good guy, but there were no sparks. We had no obvious reason to keep in touch, but we started emailing anyway; it felt like the polite thing to do. We eventually found solace in sharing our separate lives with each other. We became such good friends that we thought we should go on a second date a whole year later.

Remember Meg Ryan and Tom Hanks in *You've Got Mail*? Two people fall for each other over email. That was us. We dated long distance for a bit, and then I moved to LA; we got engaged and then married.

On paper, we had everything going for us. Two hard-working, intelligent people with similar values and morals. Our parents immigrated to the United States for a chance at a better life. We both had engineering degrees from excellent universities. I looked around and compared to everyone around us, we seemed to be checking off all the boxes. We set goals to keep us moving toward what I thought would be the inevitable—having kids and growing our family unit.

We'll get out of debt.

We'll buy a starter home.

I'll get my engineering license.

He'll get a better job.

I had heard that the number-one cause of arguments was money, so we vowed never to argue over money and found a way to actually honor that. Because we were both Taiwanese, we never had to explain family cultural expectations to each other.

Holidays felt easy to navigate. We were both able to understand the extended family balancing act, allowing us to avoid holiday landmines. We were on the same page in terms of religion. He was smart and loyal. We went on dinner dates and volunteered together. We participated in marriage mentoring through our church for five years, during which we were shepherded by more mature couples. We did the right things, but something was always amiss.

We even had a decent sex life until the end, when the inner turmoil poured over into our intimacy and everything dried up. After sex disappeared for a year, we started going to couples' therapy. Looking back, that was an obvious symptom of bigger underlying problems. Neither one of us really wanted to rock the boat too much, which meant that we ignored that there was a serious problem. I certainly wasn't completely honest about where I was in those therapy sessions.

And we argued. I remember one time Ben asked me if I thought perhaps we argued too much. "Of course, not!" I said vehemently. "Everyone argues." But I don't think it was the arguments—it was the undercurrent that troubled us. I didn't want to face whatever it was that I was feeling.

I wasn't ready to consider leaving. I couldn't even imagine it. I had made a vow and believed that marriage was forever. I didn't believe in divorce, and neither did the church we had married into. The church doctrine equated divorce with leaving God and the church. If I wanted to leave Ben, I'd be ostracized by the congregation and my church friends, who were the only friends we had.

After a year of couples' therapy, I finally turned to private therapy. It made me feel better, but I still couldn't decide exactly what was wrong in the relationship.

When we separated, Ben still had hope that it could work. I sometimes wished I was different. I wished I was the person who could stay. Why couldn't I just be happy with what I had? Why did I need or want more? Why couldn't I have been a simple girl with simple dreams, happy and content with simple things? What was it that drove me to think there was more? Was I being overly idealistic? Didn't I already have so much to be grateful for? The guilt made it so that I couldn't bring myself to fully leave. And then, after a year of living separately passed, I realized I also couldn't make myself go back. The decision had been made at some very deep subconscious level. It took my conscious mind many years to catch up to that realization.

When I finally told Ben I wanted to file for divorce, he begged me not to. I couldn't see a road back, but I waited to file, in case I changed my mind. I had a hard time feeling confident about my decision. I certainly never felt like I had a clear path forward.

Then, ten years after we split, I trained as a life coach with the Martha Beck Institute (MBI) Coach Training. Every tool was extraordinary and eye-opening. I kept thinking, "What if I had this knowledge back when I was with Ben?" Things would have been different. The way I had learned to navigate relationships growing up meant they tended to drag out, especially the "should I leave?" part. I never knew what questions to ask myself. I was asking myself the wrong questions and coming up empty-handed.

I began coaching others, and I also integrated all the life coaching tools I learned into my own life. Suddenly, it was like all the missing pieces of the puzzle were given to me and the process became clear. I had engineered a new outcome. When I applied the method to my own life, the struggle disappeared.

One of my clients, Amanda, is a forty-three-year-old architect and designer. She was married for five years in her twenties and never had any kids. Despite wanting to get married again, she had not been in a relationship that made it clear to her that she should. She came to me wondering if she should leave her current relationship with her boyfriend, Ken, or not. I designed the CLEAR ME process to provide clarity during a time that is often clouded by confusing emotions and contradictory thoughts. Not only did the CLEAR ME process give her all the information she needed, but she also had complete closure because the path was loving and kind.

Before, my clients would come to me to advance in their careers, which I was ecstatic to champion. But the women who came to me stuck on what to do about their relationships, it was the elephant in the room. This book became a labor of love. You don't have to suffer and wonder if you are wasting your time while you figure out if you should leave your relationship or not. You can absolutely make a decision free from guilt and fear. You'll also experience so much more ease once you stop torturing yourself with doubt and uncertainty. This is the book I wish I had all those years ago with Ben. It's the book I'm proud to have you be part of now.

Chapter 3:

Making the Right Choice

Like Megan in Chapter 1, you've been struggling with wanting to leave your relationship and feel unsure of yourself. You find yourself coming back to the same question, "Should I leave this relationship or not?"

There's no abuse or truly bad behavior, but it's also not particularly rewarding. On the surface, things are stable. You think about leaving, but what if getting out isn't any better than what you have now? Maybe it's better to just accept an okay, not-bad relationship than risk a worse one. Is this really what your life has come to, dear one?

The CLEAR ME process will guide you to create a clear path forward. This book will be your compassionate companion as you learn a new way of making decisions. In Chapter 4, I will show you how to Connect with your soul and get super clear on the top qualities of your best self, who you are when you have all the love you want and need. You'll finally be able to make a decision free from guilt and fear.

In Chapter 5, I'll teach you how to Lead with love and set a powerful intention that will put a stop to the doubt and uncertainty. Then, I'll teach you how to Engage your body in the decision-making process in Chapter 6. You've been trying to rationalize with your mind whether you should stay or leave. Here, you'll learn why that's one of the worst things you can do. It's actually keeping you stuck in a cycle of indecision.

You'll also learn how to Accept your feelings and embrace your emotions, which will open your heart to new possibilities in Chapter 7. In Chapter 8, I'll teach you how to Reframe your thoughts. You'll become aware of how your thoughts and beliefs are affecting your relationship. Once you have these foundational tools, you can move into Chapter 9, Making your conversations matter. You'll be able to show up confidently and speak up in your relationship.

Finally, in Chapter 10 we'll Elevate the accountability factor. You'll learn how to hold yourself and your partner responsible for your own outcomes.

The pinnacle of this process is what I call A Best Day, which we arrive at in Chapter 11. By this point, dear reader, you will have all the information you need to evaluate whether you're ever going to get what you need from the relationship. You have all the tools to create the exact conditions to be confident in your decision.

Most books like this will encourage you to read each chapter and do the exercises at the end of each chapter before moving on. I recommend the exact opposite. Read this book from beginning to end, all the way through. Don't stop to do the exercises until you've read through entirely. You're trying to make a decision that impacts how you feel about the life you live, and that will become a domino for many other choices you may or may not make. Why waste more time? See if this method in its entirety is for you. You can decide when you get to the end whether or not you want a holistic solution.

The exercises in the book are helpful on their own, but a piecemeal solution is limited at best. This method was created to provide answers and reassurance that will satisfy your whole being—mind, body, heart and soul. If that's the kind of solution that interests you, read forward, dear one. Let's dive into the CLEAR ME process for a clear heart and a clear path forward!

Chapter 4:

Connect to Your Soul

This chapter will help you connect with your soul and understand who you are when you are at your best in your relationship. This is who you are when you have all the love you could possibly want or need. When you are not living a life that reflects the values that resonate with who you truly desire to be, you won't be sure you are making the right decisions. Is it the other person who is wrong for you? Or are you merely conveniently blaming another human being for your inability to be true to yourself? So it's time to begin the unfamiliar but essential task of unearthing what your soul desires for you.

Best-Self Visualization
Let's dive right in and begin with a ten-minute visualization and a brief writing exercise. First, find a quiet

and private space. You need to clear your mind and bring yourself to a calm emotional state. Close your eyes and take a few deep breaths. If you are sitting, place both feet on the ground and imagine the oxygen traveling to your toes. Slowly move up through your feet and legs as you continue to breathe. Focus on each of your body parts—your knees, your thighs, and then your hips and stomach. You will probably notice different sensations as you continue to breathe. Allow yourself to be aware of these sensations.

You don't have to do anything, like try to figure out what you are feeling or even force yourself to feel differently. Just breathe and imagine oxygen traveling to each of these sensations. Continue to move up to your lungs, chest, and heart. Notice your shoulders, arms, elbows, wrists, hands and fingertips. Come back to your neck and keep breathing. Notice your jaw, your mouth, your cheeks, your eyes, and your forehead. Now that you've had a chance to focus on your physical being, your mind is clearer than before. Take a breath and make a wish for a perfect, ideal day.

Keep your eyes closed and imagine a big clock with hands next to a huge calendar on the wall. Imagine the hands moving. Suddenly they begin to spin faster. As the hands speed forward, the pages on the calendar begin to flip. Imagine the clock spinning and the calendar pages flipping until they land on a day in the future—your perfect, ideal day in your ideal relationship.

Imagine the clock returns to its normal speed and picture yourself waking up on this perfect, ideal day. Notice your surroundings and watch how the day unfolds. When you reach the best part of the day, stop and really take it in … the sounds, smells, taste, sights. Imagine that you have all the love you could ever possibly want and hope for. Notice how you blissfully dissolve into it and how it feels—the texture of this beautiful love, the way you feel in your own skin. Notice the way your heart feels, how clear your mind is. Now, I want you to notice everything about yourself. What you do. What you say. Who you are. I want you to see and remember these qualities about yourself. This is your soul telling you who you are when you are at your best. This is who you long to be every day. Savor what it feels like to be this woman.

You have reached the end of this visualization. Immediately after coming out of the visualization, write down these qualities. Memorize the top three. You will refer back to these whenever you feel lost or uncertain.

I recommended this exercise to my client, Tina. Tina is a vibrant divorced mother of two girls. She joined one of my group challenges because she felt stuck and frustrated but knew she wanted more for her life and felt therapy wasn't doing much for her anymore. She was holding on to an idea of her ex-husband so tightly that she was missing out on a real relationship. She decided that she needed to let go of her ex-husband, as well as being too busy, cluttered, and stressed. When Tina did the visualization exercise, she saw that her best-self is generous, present, warm, soft, curious, creative, passionate, encouraging, hopeful, and funny. When Tina gets stuck and doesn't know what to do, she can ask herself what would the most generous, present, and warm version of herself do? And she will know the answer because what she experienced in the visualization is her soul in its most loving and complete state.

If you want to decide whether you should leave this relationship, this is how you want to do it. All your confusion has you currently spinning in circles. But this process allows you to approach your decision from a place of complete love, not fear or guilt. Are you ready to take on the challenge?

Now, in all of Tina's interactions, she's going to channel her best self. She will be generous, present, warm, soft, curious, creative, passionate, encouraging, hopeful, and funny. As she strives to embody the woman she saw in her visualization session, she will be able to see and experience her relationships through a new lens. People will now be interacting with a woman who is generous, present, and warm. It gives her relationships the best possible chance to flourish. If they don't flourish when she's at her very best, there's not much that can fix that.

Remember Amanda from Chapter 2? I guided Amanda through the best-self visualization and this is what we learned. When Amanda is her best self, she's optimistic, passionate, curious, adventurous, and kind. When confronted with questionable behavior in the past, she was quick to label them as red flags. And once a red flag was labeled as such, it became a very difficult uphill battle for the other person to prove themselves worthy of her affection. It's hard to say if those relationships didn't work out because the other person was really guilty of what she thought the red flag indicated, or perhaps the other person merely got tired of constantly proving themselves and stopped trying. After the exercise, she decided she was going to be more optimistic and give Ken the benefit of the doubt. He at least deserved the chance to explain how he might see things differently. And Amanda decided she could treat these occasions with curiosity instead of judgment.

Before you can leave, you deserve to find out if your relationship can blossom when you are your true self. You want to be sure that whatever is weighing down your soul isn't something that will just follow you into future relationships. Your feelings about your relationship are a wake-up call from your soul to return to your most loving self. Hold on for the amazing journey.

When Tina started her journey toward becoming more generous, present, warm, soft, curious, creative, passionate, encouraging, hopeful, and funny, she felt apprehensive.

If I'm generous, what if I'm taken advantage of?

If I'm present, who's going to take care of all the details for tomorrow?

If I'm warm, and I face a cold shoulder, won't that sting?

If I'm soft, how will I protect myself from being hurt?

If I'm curious, will I face rejection?

If I'm creative, where will I find the resources to support that?

If I'm passionate, what if that leads me somewhere else?

But what's the alternative? Be stingy so no one will take advantage? Keep hanging on to the past or projecting into the future and missing out on loving today? Be cold and unhappy? Be hard and unyielding? Never venture, never gain? Let creativity shrivel up to become stagnant? Stay reserved and miss out on sheer ecstasy?

This process of becoming your most loving self will help you determine if this is a relationship that feeds your soul or destroys it. If you can stay and be your best self, you will find yourself with a partner who is grateful because you got better with time. If your best self is met with unbearable resistance, the only way to stay is to make peace with being a hollow shell—a shadow. You need to become the person who creates the kind of love you experienced in your ideal day visualization. You might be tempted to think that if you only found that kind of love first in another person that you could finally relax and be your wonderful loving self. On the contrary, you need to do the work of becoming the person you saw, your best self, which in turn will attract the kind of love that a person of that high-loving caliber would naturally be with. You might find that love in your current relationship or you might find that you need to leave the relationship to stay true to your most loving best self. If that part of you dies, you'll feel like your soul is dying.

Another example—Jenny and Mike had been together for five months when I guided Jenny through this exercise. She had a powerful revelation—if she had all the love she wanted, she wouldn't be afraid to leave the relationship she was in. She wanted a serious relationship with a future. Mike wasn't able to talk about a future and that wasn't really what she wanted. She saw that her best self was powerful. In service to her best self, she became fearless. She didn't make any demands or give any ultimatums. She merely stated what she was missing from the relationship and ended things gracefully. She never knew when they would see each other next, and it made her feel insecure, which she no longer was willing to feel. Mike had always been smitten, but now that he saw her in her power, he suddenly had to meet her raised bar or lose her. It was as if the power of her most loving self activated the most caring parts of Mike's most loving self. He came back to her after a month and was ready to lay out the next six months. He said to her, "As much of my future that I know, we have it scheduled out." He addressed every concern that she had, and they were able to enter the next phase of their relationship.

This is how you make a decision free from guilt or fear. You will be making a decision from love, the most loving decision possible. Your best loving self.

Your best self is the person you need to be in order to be happy with yourself. When you're happy with yourself, you can evaluate your relationship with true compassion. Your soul will feel free.

Chapter 5:

Lead with Love

The purpose of this chapter is to help you lead with love so you can be your best. In order to do that, you will need to set an intention that reflects your best and true self for all your interactions in your relationship. This is the quality you will bring to the process as opposed to the desired outcome, because you can't really control how other people react or respond. I call this creating the love bubble. In many ways, your partner has been interacting with a shadow of your best self.

When Amanda is her best self, she's optimistic, passionate, curious, adventurous, and kind. She had to decide how to be those things for herself. She took up a lot of hobbies like whitewater rafting, rock climbing, and snowboarding.

Creating the Love Bubble

When Amanda was with Ken, she mostly loved how at ease she felt when she was around him. The chemistry felt effortless. He was easy to talk to. But he wasn't as chivalrous or generous as any of her past boyfriends. They would walk into a teashop, café, or coffee shop. If he wasn't going to consume anything, he would take a step back when she got to the counter. Most of their date nights were at home, and they hardly ever ate together. He would arrange to meet her after he ate, which meant she would have to find a way to eat beforehand, too. She'd never encountered such a limiting environment. If he was at her place and it was mealtime, she would offer him something to eat. If she was at his place, he would offer her water. Was this an indicator of his available time, energy, and emotional bandwidth?

Her immediate response was to write him off as stingy and cheap. But when she thought about her best self, she gave people she cared about the benefit of the doubt. He explained that he lived on a fixed budget as a creative freelancer since he had experienced some large periods of uncertainty.

She listened to his story of what it felt like to grow up with a dad who complained about his business sales every day and made him feel like they were constantly on the brink of being destitute. Understanding this, now when he would take a step back or not offer to pitch in when they were out with her friends, she decided to not take it personally. When he asked what she wanted for Valentine's Day, she asked for rose gold earrings and he got her a pair. When he asked her what she wanted for her birthday, she asked for a weekend getaway. He booked one night away. She learned that she would always have to be explicit with him. She'd always gotten fancy dinners, weekend getaways and jewelry before and never had to ask. "When I'm at my best, I'm appreciative," she told herself.

She created her own version of a love bubble. At the end of their relationship, Ken told her he had never done any of the things he did for her before. He'd never traveled with anyone, gone to Napa, bought jewelry. He was forty-five. He might have gone his whole life without those experiences. It wasn't enough for Amanda to stay, but she felt certain he had done his best.

Amanda's Last Date with Ken

Ken was in a state because he was worried they would get to the outdoor theater late and end up with a really crappy spot. He wanted to be in line at 4:30 p.m. She was on her way to his place, and he started getting frantic. By the time she saw him, he was pretty high strung. He let her into the garage to park her car and then got in his car without opening her door. It wasn't feeling very date-like. In his angst, he'd forgotten the intent of a date, which is to spend connected time, encouraging one another. And then he started complaining about what might happen: "We might end up siting on the sidewalk instead of the grass; we might end up really far from the screen where it would be hard to see; we might end up in the sun."

Amanda wanted to tell him to stop his bellyaching; it was very unattractive. But she remembered the love bubble concept. If he was agitated, how could she turn that around? She put her hand reassuringly on his arm to break the negative chatter and said calmly, "Hey, we're on our way. What will be will be, and we'll deal with it when we get there." He went silent. She wasn't sure if he actually felt any better. But she sure did. She needed to preserve her good mood by protecting her optimism.

She was determined to not let him ruin her good mood. He dropped her off to hold a place in line while he parked the car. It was only a few minutes after 4:30, and they were one of the first people in line. They were able to wait in the grass, off the sidewalk and in the shade. And since they had such a great spot in line, they also had a prime spot in front of the movie screen once the event organizers opened the doors at 6:00 p.m. to let the audience in to find spots. None of his concerns had come to pass. Amanda was relieved that they had not spent a single extra second fretting over them.

Some of his negative energy was still hanging around, but she tapped into her best self quality of curiosity. She had a few interesting things on her mind to talk about and just chatted away. At some point, he seemed to come around and join her in the present. None of those bad things that he was projecting had actually come to pass. Amanda was able to protect the intention of what she believed the date could be about. She wanted to bond and connect, so she had to put up a little force field around herself. It's the reason she spoke up in the first place.

Before she had learned about using her best qualities to create positive intentions, she might have just clammed up. Or alternatively, shouted, "Why don't we just forget about this?!" It ended up being a funny and romantic night. They got back to the car, and he got in. He didn't open her door, which she would have really enjoyed. But as her best self, she decided to focus on the positive. He had picked up some chips, guacamole, and grapes. He'd gotten the tickets and the picnic blanket and chairs. That was what he had the bandwidth for that night.

Setting the Intention

You know why people get dogs? Because dogs love you and are always happy to see you. And if there was any neglect on your part yesterday, they've forgotten and are just happy about being with you today. People aren't pets, but it is a nice lesson. Of the people you most look forward to seeing, who on that list always looks disinterested or displays immediate annoyance when they see you?

But think back to your best self and ask, *What would my best self do?* If you're not sure, narrow it down to the top three. Let's take a look at Amanda's date with Ken, for example.

Amanda's intention for a date with Ken was to be encouraging and connect. So instead of going down the road of focusing on what she didn't like, she stayed positive and was able to foster a warm connection. Overall at the end of the date, both parties could honestly say that they were encouraged and had a nice time.

To further illustrate how to set an intention, remember Tina from Chapter 4? What if Tina had been on that date with Ken instead? How could she apply her best self qualities to that situation? Tina could choose a generous, present, or warm response.

Let's take a look at how she might apply those had she been on that date with Ken. If Tina had set an intention to bring a generous spirit, she might have brought something to share, perhaps some charcuterie. Or perhaps she could have been more generous with her compliments and thanked Ken more intentionally for the snacks he brought to share.

If her intention was to bring presence, she might have focused on the perfect weather, the relatively balmy night. She could have been more vocal to point out how lucky they were in the grass, or in the shade, or in the front viewing row.

If her intention was to bring warmth, she might have handled Ken in the car with a little extra softness. Perhaps an "I'm sorry you seem stressed, but no matter what we encounter when we get there, I get to spend time with you, which is what I really wanted anyway."

What about you? What are your best qualities? Who are you when you have all the love that you could possibly need and want? How can you become this person? How would you apply it if you had been on that date with Ken instead of Amanda? You choose how you want to express the specific qualities you experienced in the visualization in that particular situation.

Here's the thing—you can't do this wrong, because your best self knows exactly what to do and how to behave. In Amanda's case, creating the love bubble was not reliant on Ken. He was anxious, worried, and complaining. But she decided to be encouraging anyway. It was the quality she intended for the date and the quality she committed to bringing to the interaction. It honored her best self. It had the effect of a more positive outcome, but had she gone in focused on how he was being a negative Nancy, she would have just been reacting. This would have been a shadow version of her. We're always responsible for how we respond. And you will always know when you are not your best self. Even if Ken never left his anxious and worried state, Amanda would still have a better time being encouraging rather than joining Ken and complaining. Even if your partner never changes, you will actually be happier with yourself.

This is how you'll stop torturing yourself with doubt and uncertainty. You won't have time for that. You'll be setting intentions that reflect your best qualities. You'll be too busy leading with love.

Chapter 6:

Engage Your Body

This is how you evaluate if you're ever really going to get what you need from the relationship. This chapter is about engaging your body in the decision-making process. You will learn to scan your body for physical sensations in response to your relationship. This will help you evaluate if you're ever really going to get what you need from the relationship.

Your Essential Self

I want to introduce you to the concept of your essential self. You may be asking me who or what this is. If you had told me back when I was a civil engineer that I would be writing a book talking about connecting with your soul, love bubbles, and essential self, I would have laughed. Loudly. Back in those days, I thought the best way to make a decision was by being rational. I made a lot of lists. My list for staying with my husband, Ben, looked like this.

Reasons to Stay

- He's Taiwanese, which my parents love.
- We understand each other's cultures.
- He comes from a good family.
- I like his family, especially his mom. I admire how much she did for the family.
- He's well-educated, working on his second master's.
- He's intelligent and his family is brilliant—his sister is one of those valedictorians who double-majored at Harvard. Mom has a lot of initials after her name. Dad has a large number of patents.
- We could have smart kids.
- We made vows.
- We share similar values and morals.
- He's a faithful Christian.
- We belong to the same church, where we got married.
- The church doctrine does not allow its members to divorce, so if I did leave, I would no longer be a member.
- We have a great friend circle in our church of other young married couples.
- These are all his friends that I adopted after moving to LA from Texas, so I wouldn't have any friends if I left.

- We both have good, stable jobs.
- I helped him make a move to working at USC.
- He supported me while I got my professional engineering license in California.
- We paid off all our debts together; they were largely mine from college.
- We never argue about money.
- Despite having different priorities, we have learned to create a budget together. He has money for his tech toys and I have money for my clothes.
- He is kind.
- He is my best friend.
- He is loyal to a fault.
- As a team, we have managed to buy our first home in the expensive LA real estate market.
- As a team, we have leveraged up and moved up to our dream home—or at least it was my dream home.

Reasons to Leave

- He is messy and disorganized.
- He lacks discipline.
- He could stand to be in better shape.
- He has terrible allergies.
- He can be a bit of a martyr, helping others to the point that he and our relationship suffer.

But after a few years together, he was less messy, more organized, and in better shape. With my help, he was taking better care of his body. And he got better about setting boundaries that protected our time together as a couple. So, the fact that he was willing to work on himself—that's really a positive.

I was having a hard time explaining how miserable I was, despite having everything we wanted and worked for. And you would probably look at that list and say, "Stay." It makes no sense. And that's how I felt, so I kept staying.

Now I want to explain the concept of your social self and your essential self, which I first learned about from my time at the Martha Beck Institute (MBI). Your social self has many voices: your parents, your family, your culture, and your society. We receive a steady stream of messages— more like a constant barrage—that never ends. We do many things to satisfy our social self.

Your essential self is who you are at your core. But how do you determine what it's trying to tell you if you've been listening to your social self all this time? This will sound ludicrous the first time you hear it, but your body holds all the information.

The Wisdom of the Body

Your mind is a tool that is at its best use in service to your essential self, but it's not great for making decisions. Left on autopilot, you'll naturally create a life listening to your social self. This makes perfect sense: these can easily be the loudest voices in your life.

Let me explain further. We are all made up of energy, and our physical bodies are containers for that energy. The physical sensations that you experience carry information. This is where modern wisdom draws a blank. It ignores this and we ignore it to our own detriment. Look at how the traditional medical field treats symptoms of illness. There's no focus on the underlying cause. Physical ailments are messages from our body. Something is amiss.

In order for me to accomplish so many things for my social self, I frequently ignored what my body was telling me. Your essential self is constantly vibrating at its own level. When you do something that it doesn't like, the energy pattern in your body is disrupted. This disruption creates physical sensations, because your body is a physical container for this energy. It may be a tickle, an itch, or a bit of discomfort. Left without a way to correct itself and come back to equilibrium, pain or illness may occur.

When I was in college, I would frequently punish my body by overworking and under-sleeping. If I got tired midday from lack of sleep, I would power through with a workout. I collapsed finally and went to see a campus doctor. My red blood cell count was dangerously low. He said I was anemic but did not determine the cause. He said I needed a sabbatical. That sounded extreme to me. I asked him what would happen if I didn't drop my course load. He said I would die. I never told my parents or anyone what he said because it sounded so ridiculous. But I would eat a meal and then need to sleep for hours. I was tired all the time. I couldn't ignore that, because I would fall asleep right after the smallest activities. I clung to one class by sleeping for hours before and after. I eventually recovered, but this would be a lesson that would repeat itself for years.

When I was married to Ben, a couple years in I developed an all-over body rash. I called it eczema, but I was fine one day and the next day couldn't stand any kind of heat on my skin. I was photosensitive. If I was in the car and the sun hit my arm, it would sting. I had to take cold baths and showers, which felt terribly cruel. I grew up loving long, hot showers and baths. If I started sweating in the slightest, my whole scalp would become incredibly itchy. The itching was unbearable, and I would scratch until my scalp was all pink. One morning, I woke up to these rough, raised plaques on my face. I went straight to my doctor without an appointment. I couldn't imagine going in to work like that. I began a regimen of corticosteroid creams—one for my body, one for my face. Special shampoo for my scalp. I was taking cold colloidal oatmeal baths. I became dependent on the creams. Ben would help me apply them all over on a daily basis. I reasoned that I must have some adult onset skin condition. I was frustrated, but it never occurred to me there might be more to it; plus, now I had medication to manage my symptoms.

Around the same time, one of my neighbors decided to train for a marathon. I decided to join her. I'm not very athletic. And I can tell you with hindsight, I absolutely hate running. After I hit double digits in mileage, I started having knee and ankle problems. I went to a podiatrist for shoe insoles. I went to a physical therapist for all the weird things coming up. I wasn't running because my body likes running. I was running because it was a physical expression of the energy moving around in me. I practically jumped at a chance to work in Thousand Oaks, which was fifty miles one way, at least an hour drive in the morning and two on the way back home. Three hours a day in a car—I was running away every chance I got.

But I never made the connection, because my social self needed the validation and it clung to the list. I couldn't find a way to express why the relationship was clashing with my essential self because I didn't know that it was. But my body held that information. When I became a life coach, I was finally able to put all of that together. If it weren't for my family, church, friends, or what I thought my society and culture valued, I would have been able to walk away. But it wasn't, because there wasn't anything wrong with my husband. As you can see, he was a human being who snored, farted, and pooped like every other human being. He could be sentimental and overly emotional, but he was not a good match for my essential self.

This next exercise is so simple it will astound you. You will want to reject my expertise and dismiss it as an unreasonable way to figure out how to leave an important relationship that has, from the outside, no obvious flaws—a decision that will affect the rest of your life. But somewhere deep down you know that what I'm saying is true.

Get out of your head with the silly unending lists and trying to give weight to what you think might be important to your social self. Here's how to give in to the wisdom of your essential self.

Remember the breathing and grounding exercise from Chapter 4? This is very similar.

The Future Test

You're going to imagine a future where you stay. Close your eyes. I want you to picture the clock with the hands next to the calendar with the pages on the wall. You will see the current time and today's date circled. Now imagine the hands start spinning and the pages flipping. They will come to a sudden stop ten years from now. Your partner is still in your life and the two of you are still together. Take a quick peek at the time on the clock. I want you to notice what you are wearing, what you are doing, any smells, sounds, sights, tastes. Notice the temperature.

You are 100 percent transported and fully in that moment. Now you will scan your body for physical sensations. Keep your eyes closed and bring attention to your feet. Start at your toes; move up to your heels, ankles, calves, knees, thighs, hips, stomach, chest, and shoulders. Notice any sensations in your arms, elbows, hands, and fingertips. Come to your neck. Allow your attention to move through your face, jaw, mouth, nose, eyes, and forehead. You have scanned your body for physical sensations. Make a mental note of what you noticed. Then open your eyes and write down the texture, temperature, color, pressure, or image of the most noticeable physical sensation. You'll notice I'm not asking you what you think or about your emotional state. These are physical sensations. Then on a scale from minus ten to plus ten, rate that physical sensation, with minus ten being nothing could be worse, like being burned alive or tortured without pain medication. Plus ten would be the best feeling possible, nothing could be better. Write down this number. It's information.

Then do the exact same exercise, but imagine a future where you leave. Start again with your eyes closed. See the clock with the hands and the calendar with the pages on the wall. Notice the current time and today's date. The hands will start spinning and the pages will start flipping. But this time, somewhere along the way, you leave your relationship. Time passes and your life settles in. You are now living a life without the man you decided to leave. The pages stop flipping and the clock returns to normal. I want you to notice the time on the clock and the date on the calendar.

Take a look at yourself, notice what you are wearing, what you are doing, notice any smells, sounds, sights, taste. Pay attention to how you feel. You are 100 percent transported and fully in the moment. Now you will scan your body for physical sensations as you did before. Keep your eyes closed and bring attention to your feet. Start at your toes, move up to your heels, ankles, calves, knees, thighs, hips, stomach, chest, shoulders. Notice any sensations in your arms, elbows, hands, fingertips. Come to your neck. Allow your attention to move through your face, jaw, mouth, nose, eyes, and forehead. You have scanned your body for physical sensations. Make a mental note of what you noticed. Then open your eyes and write down the texture, temperature, color, pressure or image of the most noticeable physical sensation. This is not what you think about the physical sensation or about your emotional state. These are physical sensations; try to give them a name. Then on a scale from minus ten to plus ten, rate that physical sensation: minus ten being the worst; plus ten being the best. Write down this number.

The goal is not to see if one scored a minus ten and the other scored a plus ten. The process allows you to see two numbers that correlate to a physical sensation in your body, and those numbers are a way to give you information from your essential self.

Some of the names that people have used to describe physical sensations in their body:

- broken glass in the stomach
- heavy brick on the chest
- knotted rope in the shoulders
- soft flowers on the heart
- yellow sunshine on the forehead
- thick rubber band in the jaw
- hard ball in the calf
- red fire in the abdomen
- fluffy cotton in the ear

- tiny hammer at the temple

As you can see, these physical sensations are not, "I think my spouse is a good provider" or "I feel sad when we argue." These are ways that you might describe a physical sensation to a small child.

Your Daily One Hundred Units of Energy

Let's go back to the concept of your body being a physical container of energy. Everyone has the same one hundred units of energy to expend each day. It's a combination of your physical, mental, and emotional energy. Let's say you go to a great party with two of your friends, Amanda and Susan. Afterward, everyone leaves. You had a great time, but you can't wait to go home and wash your face. Amanda wanted to keep the good times rolling. So she stays with a few people she met at the party, and they wander to a nearby bar. Susan unexpectedly runs into her ex. She seems fine but you get a text from her later that she has a stomach-ache and wants to cancel on brunch the next morning. That party had a different effect on each person.

Let's say it took twenty units of your energy to go to that party, sixty of Susan's, and five of Amanda's. If you are looking at this from the outside or a social self-perspective, this party took one hour of everyone's time. But if you're speaking to the essential self, you spent about eighty units of your essential energy that day at work and home. You had twenty left to give and the party took the last of it. Amanda also spent about seventy-five units of energy at work. She's a natural extrovert and the party took only five units out of her. In fact, she still has twenty units left to give. Susan loves her job the most, and it only ever takes about fifty units of her energy. But today she was at a party where she put on a smile and forced herself to have a good time so as not to spoil anyone else's good time. She's a good friend and took one for the team. But it took all she had to give and then some.

The beauty of honoring your essential self is you don't have to diagnose what's wrong with the relationship, but you can still know if you should leave or not. You can spend a lot of money on therapists to give you answers or diagnose conditions. But let me be clear: that is to satisfy your social self, the part of you that needs the social validation that you are doing the right thing by coming up with socially acceptable reasons. But your body knows if you're willing to listen to this unlikely source of information. It's just counter to what we know and honor in this society.

If you ask me today, my mind has come up with a socially acceptable reason that I left my marriage, because honestly it makes people feel better to have a reason that satisfies their own social-self view of the world. And I share it because it feels true. It took me ten years to put words to it. But it was true before I could put words to it or explain it.

The Cost of Your Social Self

At the time I was deciding whether to leave my marriage, when I would picture a future together, it would come up blank. But the sensation in my body, in my legs—the antsy tingling when I need to run away—that was there. I didn't know how to measure it or assign a number. I didn't know what to do with it. Instead, we spent thousands of dollars on therapy. We did a workbook together. We went to marriage counseling within our church and spent even more time learning about the five love languages.

It worked in the sense that we learned to communicate better. We fought less. I still love the skills I learned from the five love languages and apply them almost daily. But none of those things changed the fact my essential self was suffering in that relationship. I could never explain why I would question the validity of a relationship with so much apparent good in it. In some ways, all that therapy and time spent in counseling, reading books, and doing worksheets served my social self. It made me feel better because I didn't believe in divorce. I needed to see myself do everything to make it work. If you told me that I could have it figured out in a few months, I would have refused. It would feel like cheating somehow. Can I really just say my essential self has the answer? It's also an unhealthy cultural expectation placed on women that we should be the ones to stick things out. Until recent history, women did not have a choice in the matter. Ben and I separated after all the couples therapy, church marriage counseling, books, and worksheet exercises. Then I spent thousands more on individual therapy for a year. I was grateful to have someone consistent to talk to, with everything else happening in my life. But had I known that the type of coaching I needed was available, I could have moved forward so much faster. I'd like to share the estimated financial cost. Let's run some numbers by estimating that one hour of professional services equals one hundred dollars. It was actually more but let's use these numbers to simplify the math of what it was costing me monetarily to figure out if I should stay in my marriage or not.

We went to couples therapy for a year, roughly fifty weeks. That's $5,000 (it was actually more). Then I did individual therapy for a year, another $5,000 (it was actually more). The church marriage counseling led by a couple that had been married longer was free, but let's give the time a monetary value of $200, we met roughly every other week. So $200 times twenty-five is another $5,000. That's $15,000, and I'm not going to include the time Ben and I also spent on our own reading and doing workbooks. We were both well paid professionals—so much time and energy was spent by all involved. There was also the opportunity cost of not spending that time instead on recreation, hobbies, making the world a better place—something more rewarding. And while I made my company money at my professional rate, by the time taxes and all got covered, I was probably working a few hours every week for years to pay for solving my problem: should I leave my relationship?

Back to the one hundred units of energy. A good portion of my life during those years was spent trying to figure out a clear path forward. It never materialized. Because I was so concerned about my social self, once I finally decided to leave, I let the whole thing drag on for ages. I let the values of my social self keep me in guilt and shame. Ben didn't want the marriage to end. But I'm not sure if that was his social self or essential self speaking. What I do know is that the entire year we were separated, I didn't hear from him. I was grateful for the space because I couldn't get the voices out of my head. My marriage served my social self but it did not match my essential self.

I have some regrets about the way things ended. I wish I had a good coach back then, but I didn't know coaching was a real thing that real people did. You have the answers within you right now and a good coach can help you reflect that to yourself. But I want to say I have never regretted leaving. Staying was taking up vast amounts of my one hundred units. I improved my life by eating better, exercising more, developing hobbies—all to increase my available essential energy.

I can probably make a case that because of Ben's upbringing, we were creating the same pattern of his parents, where his mom gave too much and was overstressed and his dad was clueless, but does the reason really matter? If you're supposed to be together, does it matter why? If you're not meant to be together, does it matter why? Isn't it better to make the best decision for you and begin moving forward?

Katie is a beautiful single mom who got married to a great guy when her teen son was in high school. Katie left her seemingly perfect husband because she felt disrespected by the attention he gave other women. And it wasn't that he initiated contact. Other women found him attractive, enjoyed his company, and would chat him up. Being a nice guy, he would not cut off the conversations that for her were a little too long and inappropriate for a married man. He never cheated on her. But he never quite understood how to make her feel safe. His behavior threatened her security, and she was at her wits' end.

We can assign fault or accept that this is who they essentially are—she, a woman who grew up watching her dad cheat on her mom, and he, a late bloomer who was finally popular later in life. Changing would take such vast amounts of energy. Is it worth it? And the moment either side relaxes, he'll be a little too receptive to a chatty gal, and she'll be a little too quick to chide, scold, or shake a finger.

You have your one hundred units of energy a day, your physical, mental, and emotional resources. They can be in service to your essential self. The beauty of this type of alignment with your essential self is that this will free you up to do so much more. When I honor my essential self, I have plenty of time to do so many things. Even the act of finally deciding to stay can free up so much mental and emotional weight. The act of deciding to leave can do that, too. Go back and look at the two scores you gave to the physical sensation of staying and leaving. What is it telling you to do?

Instead of a list, we are creating a pile of information, similar to a stack of books or a pyramid. This is the beginning of your decision pile, the foundation of whether you should stay in or leave your relationship.

Chapter 7:

Allow Your Feelings

The purpose of this chapter is to give you the freedom to allow your feelings in a healthy and mature way. You will be able to identify and embrace your feelings about the relationship you are actually in. It will help you handle the emotional burden you feel while you are figuring out what to do. Why does this matter? Well, remember those one hundred units of energy you have—let's not waste them on things that might never come to pass.

If you are suffering because you are imagining all the pain it will cause your husband or how disappointed your parents will be, it's really just a delay tactic. Staying for love and staying for fear of how it makes other people feel—those are two very different motives. And the more you hang on to things that satisfy only your social self, the more you'll erode the energy you have to love what's right in front of you with your essential self.

First, you have no way to predict exactly how people will react. I think my ex-husband resisted, which in my mind meant that he took it worse than I expected. I was hoping he would agree with me that we wanted different things. I didn't want to face a future without him, but it felt awful imagining a future together; it actually felt worse.

My parents didn't lecture me, which meant to me that they took it better than I expected. I didn't need to spend all that time wondering how everyone else would feel. But I did. In some ways it let me avoid how I felt. Do you feel angry, mad, sad, disappointed, hurt, abandoned, or enraged that you have to make this decision? It's necessary to just call out these emotions.

ACT—Acceptance and Commitment Therapy

Look in a mirror and state out loud the emotion you feel most. Then repeat, adding, "I am having the thought that I feel" before it. Then add, "I notice" in front of that statement. So, if you are angry, it will sound like this:

- I am angry.
- I am having the thought that I feel angry.
- I notice that I am having the thought that I feel angry.

Some of the emotions you feel will be so strong that you'll want to be able to catch your breath and bring some awareness to it. So, you can see yourself as a human being experiencing a perfectly normal emotion instead of one-hundred percent identifying as the emotion. Let's look at a couple of examples.

- I am sad.
- I am having the thought that I feel sad.
- I notice that I am having the thought that I feel sad.
- I feel ashamed.
- I am having the thought that I feel ashamed.
- I notice that I am having the thought that I feel ashamed.

Let's look at Megan—she has a great career. The kids are in college now. There are no big "problems." Part of her suffering is that she doesn't think her feelings are okay. I've borrowed this from ACT (Acceptance and Commitment Therapy) because it's such an effective tool for otherwise very outwardly successful individuals to allow themselves to feel their feelings instead of making themselves feel worse just for having them. She feels horrible for considering a divorce.

- I am horrible.
- I am having the thought that I am horrible.
- I notice that I am having the thought that I am horrible.

Being able to take a breath and say, *This is an emotion that I'm having*, which is a normal part of the human experience, will increase your emotional resilience. You'll need it if you decide to stay and be a loving partner. You'll need it if you decide to go through the process of a loving breakup.

Everything you do or don't do is in service to an emotion. It may appear rational, but if that were the case, given the same circumstances, everyone would make the same choices. If I gave ten people one hundred dollars, they would all spend it in different ways. And whatever they choose makes them feel better in some way. We do things to make us feel better or to prevent us from feeling worse. We eat because we don't want to feel hungry or as comfort, like emotional eating. We go to work to feel useful but also to make money, which makes you feel more secure.

I have clients who come in with all kinds of goals. I have them write down the top-ten things they would like to have in their life. Next to it, I ask them to write down how it would make them feel to have it. I'm amused when someone writes down they would like to have a million dollars because they would feel less stressed. The only reason you would be less stressed is if you learned how to become a person who manages stress better. Otherwise, you'll just have a million dollars' worth of stress to manage.

Present Emotion or Imagined Emotion

It's really important to face your emotions and decide if it's happening in the moment or you're creating a situation to be emotional about. You just got in a huge fight, your emotion is in the present and you more than deserve to feel it. You're imagining how embarrassed you'll feel when your coworkers find out you're divorced. That's your brain working overtime. It might be tempting to be mad at your social self, but it's just a side of you created to protect you from the challenges of embracing your essential self until you're emotionally ready.

There are plenty of ways to avoid how you feel and stay stuck as an emotional child. Young children often need the support of an adult to help them self-soothe. They learn to trust that help is ready, willing, and nearby. Emotional adulting means you take responsibility for your own emotions and you let others take responsibility for theirs.

Let's say Megan's parents are disappointed. Are they really the ones who have to come home every day to her husband and live with her decision? No, but she does. So why does it feel rational to stay together to keep the peace for other people? And if you're staying together for your kids, would you wish your own relationship on them? Would you want for them to feel everyday what you feel about your own partner in their own lives? What are you showing them by example about the kind of love they can expect to have?

Perhaps you're projecting your inability to deal with your own emotions on your partner. And if they really are incapable of dealing with their own emotions, your choice to stay with them says more about where you are emotionally than where they are. I wasn't that emotionally strong when I finally forced myself to leave my marriage. I made myself strong after. On the days I was sad, I cried. I also spent a lot of days at happy hours and out with friends so that I could handle my sadness in small spurts. I didn't know how to self-soothe. I wish I knew back then that I could tell myself that I made a good decision and that it was okay to be sad, that it was normal. I wish I hadn't spent so much time beating myself up about it.

Ring of Fire

I want to share the Ring of Fire exercise and how it can help you become resilient. I adapted it from a concept I read about in Martha Beck's book *Steering by Starlight*. She explains that in order to get from the "shallows" to the core of peace, there's a ring of fire we must cross. And of course the only way to get to the core is to go through the ring of fire. Staying at the edge in the shallows becomes comfortable and familiar. Our fear of the fire can keep us in relationships that bleed our soul dry. We have to face some unpleasant emotions in order to watch some false beliefs and negative thoughts go up in smoke. I know a few people who would rather climb a mountain than face difficult emotions.

Next time you feel an emotion that is a reaction to something in the present, not the distant past or the unknown future, take a seat and close your eyes. Let the emotion rise up in you. Imagine a huge fire in front of you. Normally you would step back or run away, but just stand your ground and face it. This fire is the full brunt of the emotion that you are tempted to run away from. It's all-consuming and it's right there roaring in front of you. It's so strong, it's created a gust of air around you. Breathe in deeply and slowly; feel the force in front of you.

Now imagine yourself walking right into it. Let it consume you completely and take over. Give in to it and collapse as it envelops you. Just dissolve into it wholeheartedly and sit until the emotion has passed through you. When you open your eyes, you will notice that you are alive, you are whole, and it did not kill you. You did not have to run away from your emotions; you are capable.

Ken and Amanda had been dating for two months and the holidays were nearing, so they'd arranged to do a small gift exchange. Nothing fancy or big, because it was still quite new. She had plans to see her parents for the holidays. When she asked him what his plans were, he said that he and his brother Cory were planning to fast and do a cleanse and basically be shut-ins. She was pretty mortified.

He had mentioned to her that he had just started a new job over the summer. She couldn't imagine why he would want to spend his precious few paid holidays at home with his brother, not eating and not enjoying the holiday with friends. His mom had passed away and he and his brother were estranged from their father. She had spent every long holiday she ever had on vacation traveling as far away as possible for as long as she could. She felt pretty judgmental about it, like it was a terrible thing. But she asked herself whose business she was in: Am I in my business, his business, or God's business? And she realized that it was his how he wanted to spend the holidays. Who was she to judge?

She didn't really feel close enough to him at the time to invite him to spend the holidays with her family. But she felt like she had been punched in the stomach. She was having a visceral reaction to this information. She lay on her bed, closed her eyes, and walked into the ring of fire. She allowed herself the emotion she was experiencing in its full capacity. She had no thoughts about it. She just cried.

Perhaps she was crying for him—what kind of life did he have that it would feel normal for him and his brother to be at home, not eating, not celebrating with others on his paid vacation days? Perhaps she was crying for herself, a painful acknowledgment that this person might limit her. Perhaps she was crying for them, a disappointment that a future she hoped for was unlikely. She did not need to make any decisions. She just embraced the pain. And then suddenly she stopped crying. She had let the emotion run through her body, and it released its hold on her. She never came to Ken with her judgments and holier-than-thou position of how he should have "more" life. It was no longer necessary. It also gave her the ability to be present with the best parts of him.

Somewhere along the way, your social self learned that it would be a display of weakness to show the world when you are feeling vulnerable. So, you put on a brave face and say the right things, but you just can't seem to feel better in your relationship.

In this chapter, you have two methods for dealing with your emotions. The first is to bring awareness. Perhaps you'll notice if your emotion is the result of thinking about the past or the future. If you do, use the awareness to create room for curiosity. Ask yourself, "Why would I still be feeling this way about something in the past?" or "Why would I feel this way about something that might never happen?" or "And if it did happen, do I really want to experience it more than I have to? Do I need to pretend to prepare myself? And will it really make anything better?"

If you are fully in the present, then use the ACT method. Say, "I notice I am having the thought that I feel this emotion." Does it feel better to just to have this deeper awareness? If so, then stay curious about the events surrounding the emotion and make a note of the information you are gathering. If you start to feel like you are judging or condemning your emotions harshly, or you suddenly feel ready for an argument, this is a sign you need to step into the ring of fire.

Notice that Amanda was ready to go and tell Ken that he was doing the holidays all wrong. She wanted to condemn and judge. What she really needed was to step into the ring of fire. Running away from an emotion means that it's still there in the background, and it will sneak up on you when you least expect it. You will be mid-argument and say something snarky, a bit of the flame leaping over your shoulders.

So go ahead and face it head on; there will be no bite to that argument left. She learned over time, she and Ken viewed the world quite differently and needed different things to be happy. They had clashing philosophies, but this allowed her to not constantly accuse him of living a limited life. He was content with simple things, and that served him well. If he didn't see a need to change that, what sense would it make for her to take that on?

You have the tools to identify and embrace your emotions, which means you can accept them without having to react to them. This is such a powerful skill. It also allows you to be responsible for your actions. You can feel whatever you want, and then you get to choose how you respond. This makes a difference because it means you are taking responsibility for yourself and your own happiness. It also means that you will give this gift to those around you. Your partner is responsible for how he responds. He's responsible for his own happiness.

Making Positive and Honest Requests

It's easy to get in the habit of believing that someone else is responsible for our happiness. Yes, they can contribute to it, but they aren't responsible for our happiness. Let's say you feel sad. Ask yourself what you need before you demand support from your partner. Maybe you need a kind word, so you give yourself a kind word. Then when you talk to your partner, they might give you a kind word. Since that was exactly what you needed, you can respond with appreciation. "Thank you for being kind; it's exactly what I needed." If they respond indifferently, you can express desire. "Thank you for listening; I would love a kind word right now if you have it in you." If they respond harshly, you can express your hurt. "It sounds like I caught you at a bad time; I was hoping for a kind word. Perhaps you don't have that in you right now. I need to step away for a few minutes."

Do you see how powerful it is to decide ahead of time what you need? And if you don't know, it's not really fair to villainize your partner for not knowing. It's okay to learn together, but recognize that if you don't know exactly what will make you feel better, it's not that your partner can't read your mind (even though they can't). They don't know because you don't. Sometimes you get lucky, and you're with someone who magically knows.

One time Amanda had an argument with Ken, and he was making it worse by getting defensive. She asked him if he wanted her to tell him what would make her feel better or if he just wanted to guess and figure it out on his own. He begrudgingly allowed her to tell him what she knew about herself. "It would mean a lot to me if you would say I'm sorry I hurt your feelings. That wasn't my intention and I'll do a better job communicating when my schedule changes." She watched his face as he wrestled with this and then he quoted her exactly and she felt better immediately. He gave her what she needed. She wasn't embarrassed to ask for it. She knew because she had learned to ask herself.

She mentally soothed herself and told herself it was okay for her to have her feelings. She even imagined an adult version of herself apologizing to the hurt child in her, so she knew an apology would make her feel better. You can't make someone apologize to you, but you can ask and see if they respond. She gave herself what she needed, and Ken was able to give her what she needed as well. She made the request and could have been angry that she had to ask, but that's what it takes if you want to be in a mature relationship. Open your heart to your partner by being open and honest with yourself. You can't do this if you can't even identify something like what emotion you are feeling. That allows you to figure out what you need, which allows you to figure out if this relationship will ever meet your needs.

This is the next layer of your decision pile. Add this information to the pile. What happens when you embrace your emotions fully? What happens when you make honest requests?

Chapter 8:

Reframe Your Thoughts

The purpose of this chapter is to help you reframe your thoughts so you can become aware of how your thoughts and beliefs are affecting your relationship and your ability to make a decision. I love it when smart women come to me, because they have made lists of all the reasons they should stay and all the reasons they should leave, as if a pros and cons list could answer a question that tugs at your heart and soul. But lists appear to make rational sense and are better than fretting and coming up with nothing. Herein is where the fault lies. Our minds our not the great decision-makers we think they are. Our minds are incredible at execution. But we do the opposite. We try to make decisions with our minds, which naturally resist change, and then we try to force our bodies to go along with it.

I talked about the essential self in Chapter 6 and how the body is a physical container of energy. When you take action that honors your essential self, the vibrational energy of your being is supercharged. When you go against it, it takes more of your one hundred units of energy.

For example, let's say you have a friend named Janet who is planning to take a vacation. She comes to me and we decide to use the body scan exercise to determine her physical sensation score for two possible vacation destinations. One is a first-class luxury trip to Thailand and the other, a budget economy trip to Ireland.

When she asked her friends, they all told her Thailand because of the bikini weather, the sandy beaches, the friendly people, and how far her dollar would go. Ireland would be cold and rainy and the sites would be spread out. On the surface this made a lot of sense. But when she closed her eyes and imagined herself in Thailand, she felt the heat and humidity. Her hands felt clammy and she almost couldn't breathe. It was like there was a vice closing on her throat. She rated the metal vice on throat feeling as a minus five.

Then she imagined driving around Ireland, pulling over as sheep passed on the narrow roads. She stepped out of the car and felt the coolness of the air land on her face. It was abrupt, but it made her feel sharp and alive. She noticed that her hands were relaxed and outstretched, and the sting on her face felt like a snow cone. When she tried to describe it, the color blue popped up, the same blue as the blue raspberry bubble gum flavor that was her favorite as a child. She rated the blue snow-on-face feeling as a plus eight. Yes, her social self would probably have greater validation from friends about going to Thailand; she'd get plenty of likes and comments on the colorful photos. But she'd be slightly annoyed the entire time, trying not to snap at the staff at the resort for taking too long to bring her ice because of the metal vice sensation on her throat. She could still make it great, but each day would require large amounts of her one hundred units of energy just to stay positive. She'd want to sleep in as long as possible to avoid the heat of the day and most likely still come back home feeling exhausted from her trip.

What if Janet decided to go to Ireland instead, where her essential self would be happiest? She'd get a few comments on her pics. (Oh bummer, you caught another rainy day. Why didn't you go to Thailand?) In her excitement, Janet spent all her spare time bookmarking little towns off the beaten track. She ducked into little pubs and met local musicians. She was in a fantastic mood and made fast friends every night as she shut down the bar, dancing her heart away. She couldn't wait to wake up every morning to see the next small town, where she had new friends practically heralding her arrival, since she was now part of the local friends of friends network. She barely slept but never felt tired. The energy she received fed her, since she wasn't spending all her time trying to convince herself to do anything. That blue snow sensation stayed with her every day of the trip, and before she knew it, it was time to go home. She didn't have that many pictures, but she came back completely refreshed and energized. She declared Ireland the most magical place she had ever been.

So, what does this have to do with trying to figure out if you should leave? It's an example of what it feels like to stay in a relationship that your essential self is giving you a negative score on, but you stay anyway. You can stay, but you'll spend all your mental resources making the most of it and you won't have much energy left. There's an opportunity cost. When Janet thought about choosing Thailand, she lost more than just the chance to be in Ireland: she lost the chance to feel and experience everything that came with it.

One of the coaching tools I learned from MBI was the coaching model. It teaches us that circumstances can't be changed. But our thoughts about those circumstances affect how we feel. And how we feel creates a result.

Alice is a beautiful Instagram model. Her husband, Elliot, always has this thought that he could lose her; maybe she'll meet someone else and leave him. It's more than a thought; it's a belief he has. According to his belief that she might leave him for someone else, he won't let her out of his sight. He doesn't want her to spend time with friends he doesn't approve of. He's got her phone tracking turned on so he always knows where she is. All purchase notifications on her credit cards go to his phone so he always knows what she is buying. Most of the time she's very understanding of his insecurities and enjoys the life they have together. She has often said how much she admires him, that he is the man of her dreams in many ways. About once a year, though, she'll suddenly feel suffocated by all this hemming in and will run away from home. This belief that she might leave him has now suddenly come true. His response is to tear through town looking for her. He convinces her to come home. They make their apologies.

Here's the power of that belief. Not only did he make it come true: now there is also confirmation bias. The last time she ran away, he was convinced that there was somebody in the wings; he couldn't see beyond his belief system. During the day or two that she was holed up at a friend's house, it also didn't occur to him that a little time apart might be good for them. His belief has generated feelings and the emotions are real even if the thoughts they are based on are not.

If I thought I was going to lose someone I love, I would feel sad, scared, and vulnerable. His fear resulted in all the actions I mentioned: friend, phone, and credit card tracking. The outcome was a suffocating relationship that Alice has to run away from on occasion. There could come a day that she no longer feels he is the man of her dreams. Perhaps you think this is an extreme example. Well it always feels extreme when you are on the outside. The emotions are real. The lesson here is to consider whether it's your beliefs about your relationship that are causing you to suffer.

Elliot didn't ask himself if it was true that Alice had left him. His focus was on the fact that it could be. So he spent his energy trying to prevent it from happening. What he doesn't see is that he is creating the conditions for the exact thing he fears most to happen. That's what happens when our beliefs are rooted in fear.

One thing that scares my clients from wanting to do this work is the belief that if they know the answer, they must immediately do something about it. Another thing clients often worry about is that they cannot change their mind when they learn new information. We start with the body scan and hold that information lightly. We do the ideal day and best self exercises. Some people solve their own unhappiness by becoming the most loving version of themselves.

Sometimes it's more of a domino effect: one person shows up more authentically, the other person is inspired to show up more authentically, and the pair finds themselves in a new bliss. Then we move on to emotional maturity and taking responsibility for knowing what we need for ourselves. By the time we've reached the mind-set work in this chapter, my clients are feeling very confident that the information they have is reliable and that they will soon have a complete and usable framework.

Try this thought instead: I am able to collect information to make the better decision for our relationship.

Another belief that holds people back is that exploring a life beyond the relationship is disloyal. That thought generates a feeling of guilt that then results in trying to be loyal by looking for reasons to stay. But you do the relationship a disservice by not trusting that love will prevail.

If you have any faith, religion, or philosophy that you hold, you know that periods of testing or doubt allowed you to reaffirm your belief with greater conviction, find a higher calling or let go of something you ultimately are happy to let go of. Even an atheist who grew up Catholic can say I now believe science is a higher truth. If the reasons you find to stay are rooted in guilt, eventually that will become a burden too great to bear. And it will be hard not to blame the person in front of you for "forcing" you to carry that burden. Try this thought instead: It is kinder to figure out if I should leave this relationship.

You want to stay from a place of joy, not burden. And if you go, you'll want your next relationship to be a mindful, healthy choice, not an unchecked reaction to all that was missing.

It's also okay to live for your social self. It'll take more of your energy, but if you don't have a negative body compass score you can stay for a long time. It's a choice. Instead of ruminating, turn your mind's attention to executing. Brainstorm the best possible thoughts that will make you feel better. I highly recommend hiring a coach to help you do thought work. A free resource is Byron Katie's *The Work*. These tools, along with the next chapter on transformational conversations, lay the groundwork for changing the things that you can.

One of the most difficult things about reframing your thoughts, is figuring out which ones to reframe. If it's a deeply ingrained belief, perhaps you won't even recognize that it's a thought worth reframing. Back when people believed the world to be flat, there was no reason to think, *Should I reframe this belief I have about the world being a different shape?* So how do you choose? You choose when thoughts create pain points like the ones Elliot encountered. His beliefs were true and I could not convince him otherwise, but he was not coming to me for coaching. If you are reading this book, you want something more for yourself and your relationships. You still have hope that there is more. When you experience a strong emotion, ask yourself why you feel the way you do? And then ask if what you believe is true. Ask yourself if it's absolutely true. A fact that could be verified by anyone in the world.

Amanda and Ken went on a few dates and she thought things were going well. Then Ken had to go out of town for work. When he came back, he asked her out for a drink. Amanda was unhappy. I asked her why.

"We haven't seen each other in a couple of weeks and he's not making much of an effort to reconnect."

"Is your belief that he's not making much of an effort to reconnect true?"

"Of course it is."

"Is it absolutely true?"

Amanda pondered it, but didn't want to let go of how jilted she felt. But she knew that other people might be perfectly happy with a wine date. And it was possible that this was Ken's way of making an effort to reconnect with her. He did ask to see her again after all. "Maybe it's not absolutely true."

Beliefs feel emotionally true. So the best way to approach them is to notice when you feel strongly about something. Then ask yourself what thought or belief is making you feel that way. We have many thoughts that have no emotional energy tied to them. The ones that do are beliefs. And if a belief is causing you to suffer, it's possible to reframe it. That moment you entertain the possibility that another belief might be just as true is magical.

Amanda originally had in her mind that she was not going to bother seeing Ken again because she felt insulted by his level of effort. Once she saw that it was possible that what she believed might not be true, she was able to allow space for different possibilities.

Get in the habit of noticing the thoughts underneath your feelings. Treat it as game, always asking yourself first, "Is it true?" Then, "Is it absolutely true?" It should create a sense of lightness in your life. A kind of "Alice in Wonderland" effect. If everything we believe is a matter of perspective, is there another perspective to consider that could be more pleasant to live by?

When you believe thoughts that create more positive emotions, you will see different results. If Amanda had shown up on that wine date with a chip on her shoulder or insisted that Ken do better after returning from his work trip, do you think that would have gotten her closer to what she wanted? To spend time with someone who wants to make an effort to connect with her? It would have done the opposite. He would have felt burdened by a belief that he did not share. But we create burdens and conflicts like this in our own lives because we never question our thoughts.

The ability to reframe your thoughts creates new outcomes. Amanda showed up to that date with a great attitude with the belief that Ken did indeed want to connect with her. At the end of the date, she shared how she felt, and they were able to both have a good laugh at the misunderstandings that can so easily happen as you are dating and getting to know someone. New thought, new feeling, new outcome. Try it for yourself. Find a fantastic mindset coach if you are having difficulty getting the hang of it. You don't want to miss out on having this skill.

Now you have the power to create new results in your life. When you enter into situations with beliefs that create a positive emotion, see what outcome results. You now have even more information to add to your decision pile.

Chapter 9:

Making Your Conversations Matter

The purpose of this chapter is to guide you in making your conversations matter. You will know how to show up confidently and speak up to your partner as you transform yourself.

Surprise! You've been undergoing a transformation and showing up differently than you have in the past. You know and acknowledge the best qualities of your most loving self and you strive to be your best self. You're becoming a pro at creating intentional love bubble moments. You understand more every day about what you have been doing for your social self and making a shift to focus on honoring your essential self. You're embracing your emotions and making positive requests that reflect your actual needs. Your mental energy is consumed by all this, and you don't really have the mental space to ruminate.

Do you still feel like a horrible person for wanting to leave? A committed relationship is something you wanted before you got into this, and it still seems like something worth pursuing. In this chapter, we're going to explore transparency and authenticity. Perhaps one of your best self qualities is honesty.

Remember Tina? Tina started her journey toward becoming more generous, present and warm, soft, curious, creative, and passionate in Chapter 4.

The first quality on the list is generous. As she tried to be more generous, she found that her partner, George, would do things that made her feel bad about being generous. But she came to the realization that she loved this quality in herself. It made her feel so good to find ways to be generous with her time and money that she didn't want to go back to her old ways.

She thought George would be ecstatic, but if she offered him the last piece of cake, he'd make a snide remark that she was only trying to get him fat. When she came home after volunteering her time at a homeless shelter, he chided her, "Who do you think you are now, Mother Teresa?" He'd laugh like it was a joke, but it started to trouble Tina because she felt there was an undercurrent. She was more attuned and could identify a small dig beneath the smiles. How could she address this in a generous, present and warm spirit? Her normal response would have been to be sarcastic back—just lighten the mood and not fight. But her body compass told her that she wanted to stay soft.

The Story behind the Story

The first communication tool I shared with Tina was the story behind the story. There's more to the story. George was reacting to an emotion that was coming up within him. What he said had less to do with her than how he was feeling about himself. Then I shared the basic nonviolent communication framework:

- I notice
- I think
- I feel

Remember how you learned about circumstances in the last chapter? Well, those are facts that haven't been colored by your thoughts or beliefs. For example, Kate and Tasha are meeting for dinner at 7:00 p.m. Tasha is twenty minutes late. Kate decides to say something. Which one feels like nonviolent communication to you?

- You kept me waiting? You know how busy I am. You better have a good reason.
- You're so irresponsible. I find it so annoying.
- I noticed that you're really late. I think you're being selfish. I feel like you don't respect me.
- I noticed that you arrived twenty minutes after eight. I think it's respectful to be on time. I feel a bit disappointed because I've been looking forward to this all day. I would love a heads-up in this situation.

The first one includes name-calling and a demand. This is verbally abusive. The second one includes shaming and lacks vulnerability. It's manipulative. The third one is what tends to come out when people who don't have a good conflict resolution modeled in their past start with the first time they try nonviolent communication. Let's break down each part.

I notice…a fact. A fact is something that is absolutely true. "Really late" is not a fact. "Really" is subjective. If you ever wonder if you are stating a fact, ask yourself, *Could I ask anyone in the world this question and have everyone give me the same answer?*

Even something like "I noticed you painted the door blue" might not be absolutely true because not everyone would agree it's blue. Sometimes the best thing is to keep it as short as possible. I noticed you painted the door. I noticed when you came in. These things can be verified. There is paint on the door, and the person is inside the room.

"I think you're being selfish." That's replacing a thought about what you value with a thinly veiled dig. Except it's not that thinly veiled. A thought about what you value would sound like, "I think it shows respect to ask my opinion before you decide what color to paint the house."

"I feel like you don't respect me." You're not really sharing a feeling. "You don't respect me" is not a feeling. Emotions sound like mad, sad, angry, happy, ashamed, scared, hurt, and crushed.

A calm observation sets the proper tone for nonviolent communication. "I noticed that you arrived twenty minutes after eight." It starts with a fact. If any part of this opening statement is not true, the other party will likely focus on that part of the statement and get defensive. It's a surefire way to get someone to stop listening. Next step is what you think which is a bridge from the observation to how you feel. "I think it's respectful to be on time." You are sharing a thought that reflects your values. It's your story behind the story because otherwise, what's the big deal? Then you can share how you feel. "I feel disappointed." You may or may not get an apology, but the I notice, I think, I feel method is the best way to be heard. It's a story with a beginning, a middle and an end. And by sharing in this fashion, you offer your partner the ability to see and hear your side. How else can they say, "I'm so sorry I made you feel that way"? Finally, the closing piece is a request. Sometimes that's the most difficult part because it can feel quite vulnerable. "Next time, would you mind letting me know that you're running behind?" You don't want to spend your life too scared to ask. You're afraid to ask because you're afraid of what it means if they refuse your request, which they can do. Or perhaps your fear of vulnerability shows up in the form of demands. "Never be late again!" You become a dictator. Lay your request before your partner as a peace offering. Then you get to just watch what they do. It's information that goes into your decision pile.

Remember Amanda? She confronted Ken after a series of date nights where they stayed home with no real plans. "I noticed that we stayed in on Saturday. I think making plans is a way to show somebody they matter. I feel a bit disappointed. I would love it if you put more effort into planning a date night." What she learned about Ken is that he got defensive—every time, even with the softest approach. It's one of the reasons she decided to leave. Amanda concluded, "We really enjoyed our time together, but I spent so much energy phrasing discussions that I realized I would rather use that energy in other ways."

The Punishment Does Not Fit the Crime

This tool is great for unexpected and outsized outbursts. It's a time to get curious. One time I was out with my sister Jenny for lunch. I was on a budget and ordered a dish for under ten euros. She ordered a dish for herself, an appetizer, something for her son, and then a dish at the end for takeaway. The bill came and it was a little over forty Euros. I considered my budget and asked myself what I felt was generous. I offered, "How about I give you a twenty?"

She immediately got agitated and started yelling, "Why are you nickel and diming me?"

When we got home, I approached her. "I noticed you said that I was nickel and diming you. I only ordered one thing that was under ten Euros and you ordered everything else. I thought that offering a twenty was generous. How was that nickel and diming?"

She replied, "I thought we would split the bill. But now that you say it that way, I guess not." I could see she wanted to stay angry. I could also see that the punishment did not fit the crime. It's not normal to yell at someone over a couple of Euros. Healthy circumstances dictate, "Hey, we're a bit short, do you have a couple more?" Or even, "I thought we'd split it." But when you can get curious in moments like this, you'll know you've hit the bigger story behind the story.

A little later the same day, I went to reheat the leftovers from lunch to eat for dinner, specifically the dish I ordered. I was on a video call back to the States and Jenny saw me eating and barged in to ask, "Is that the rest of it?" I nodded. She started yelling at me for being selfish and inconsiderate while I was on the video call.

I told her she was welcome to eat what she wanted and left the table to take my call in private. Despite the fact that she had her entire untouched takeaway box in the fridge, all she could see was that I was eating all the food. The punishment did not fit the crime, and there was a bigger story behind the story. I realized I was not in charge of figuring it out. I also was not responsible for her outbursts. It was unpleasant, sure, but this was not about me, and I did my best not to get into an argument. She wanted to be mad, so it would give her permission to say whatever she wanted. When you notice a huge disconnect between the cause and effect, collect that information for your decision pile.

How to Stop Nagging

Sometimes the best method is the most direct. Amanda and Ken had been together for six months. Amanda went to visit some family in Ireland over the summer and invited Ken to come out for part of her trip. He had adopted a special gluten-free diet to improve his health, which she found challenging back in Chicago, because there was a great food scene she loved to follow. She was a chef groupie but realized not everyone would share that passion. So, she planned out a menu for Ken's trip, things they could use for meal prep so they wouldn't have to eat out every day.

The first couple days she happily cooked breakfast, lunch, and dinner. Then they made their way to their first destination, Belfast. She found an apartment-style hotel with kitchens in Belfast and woke up early to meal prep. Then they spent their days on *Game of Thrones* tours, wandering around the restored waterfront by the Titanic Museum, and ducking through the alleys of one of the city's quarters.

They'd get back to the hotel and Ken would lie in bed in front of the TV while she unpacked their lunch containers and made dinner. By the second day of this, she was quite irritated. She wanted to rest too. She didn't really want to spend her whole vacation cooking for Ken while he relaxed.

At first she wanted to tell him, "I notice that you don't pitch in to help with the meal prep, even though you're the one with the dietary restrictions. It feels like the burden is on me and I'm starting to feel resentful. I'd like you to be more considerate." But now she had more information about him. He tended to get defensive. Instead of saying what she didn't like, she decided to ask for the behavior she wanted. That night after dinner, she asked him what time he wanted to get up the next day. He felt he needed about forty-five minutes to get ready. Amanda swallowed everything she wanted to say and focused on inspiring a positive outcome. Here's what she said instead: "I've been waking up an extra thirty minutes early to prep breakfast and lunch. Could you add an extra fifteen minutes to help me with the meal prep?" Every morning the rest of the trip, he stood next to her peeling eggs and slathering mustard on gluten-free sweet potato wraps. He was slower at it but he was helping and each day he got a little better. And it was bonding to do an activity together that supported both of them. Amanda could have focused on the selfish act or his inconsiderate behavior, but she made the switch to why does it bother me and what do I want instead.

Inspiring someone else means you focus on the information that the seemingly negative feelings give you. Embrace your emotions genuinely and ask, *What does this tell me?*

Becky came to me because she'd been having a series of small tussles with her boyfriend of six months, Larry. He mentioned he felt like sometimes it was hard to make her happy and he was starting to feel like tiptoeing around her because he wasn't sure what might upset her. She was worried because Larry was a great guy who cared deeply for her, but the things he was saying were starting to sound similar to some of the things her ex-boyfriend, Tyler, would tell her.

So, Becky and Larry had dinner together that night. Becky noticed that he rushed through dinner and felt hurt. It seemed like he didn't want to connect with her, and she felt pretty sensitive. Of course, I could coach her through the coaching model. The circumstance was that he ate his dinner and the pace was not leisurely. The thought she was having was that he didn't want to talk to her. This made her feel dejected and touchy. She pushed her food around and acted a bit cold. The result was that he probably ate even faster and rushed off to the gym since she wasn't particularly talkative. The outcome was that neither side probably felt all that connected.

I challenged her to inspire the outcome she wanted. How would nagging about how he behaved during dinner inspire him to show up differently? I challenged her, "You wanted his attention. So why didn't you ask for it? Don't be passive-aggressive. Put on your big girl pants and ask for what you really want. You felt hurt because you wanted to connect with him."

In the next conversation she had with Larry, she said: "Hey, I noticed we rushed through dinner a bit yesterday. Do you mind if we slow down while we eat? It's our first chance to connect after not seeing each other all day. It's probably one of the things I look forward to most each

day. Spending time with you and hearing about your day."
That's a conversation that transforms. Pushing food tepidly
around a plate hoping Larry will notice that something is
wrong and will ask why the long face? Not so much.

So, when you feel something painful or negative, ask
what information is behind that emotion. Remember the
story behind the story. Becky was afraid that Larry didn't
love her enough, so she was always looking for evidence of
that lack, or confirmation bias. She took her emotion as fact
instead of information. Once she started to see that it meant
she wanted something good, she could bravely ask for it. It
still scared her, but she was with someone who would read-
ily do anything she asked. But her old habit was to punish
her partners for not reading her mind, and she was ready to
make that change.

Left unchecked, the situation would become unbearable for both sides. Becky would quickly retreat to her
corner and story of "I'm unloved." And Larry would start
to retreat, too, because nothing seemed to make her happy.
Now, she gets to be brave and see the outcome. She has
more information to add to the decision pile.

The Rule of Threes

I suggest the rule of threes to my clients. Instead of getting
tripped up on every little thing, look for patterns. If something happens three times, then bring it up. If it only happens once, do a little thought work first. Ken and Amanda
were talking about a couple they knew. Ken remarked,

"Well, sometimes women don't know what they really want. I mean women say all these things, but look who they end up with."

Another time, Amanda brought up a conversation with a friend of hers. Ken commented, "Well, sometimes women don't mean what they say." And then another time, they had watched a movie, and his comment on the female lead was "Oh, she doesn't know what she wants." Amanda finally realized that Ken had said this enough times that he probably believed it. I asked her what she thought. Amanda thought about it. "I think women absolutely know what they want. They don't always know how to get what they want. Or perhaps they didn't believe they could really get what they wanted, so they settled for something else."

It dawned on Amanda that Ken didn't always think what women said was valid. She had been wanting him to make plans for date night; having no plans for a Saturday night felt unromantic to her. Ken had this belief that women didn't mean what they said. Well, Amanda was a woman, so perhaps he didn't always believe her. This was good information for the decision pile.

Now she had a choice to talk to him. "Hey, I noticed you saying this phrase a few times. Do you really believe that? I'm a woman who actually knows what I want and need. How do you feel about that?"

One Saturday, Ken made plans to go to a concert with Cory. They typically went about once a month. At first Amanda wondered why he hadn't ever invited her to a concert in the six months they dated. So she asked for an invite. "Hey, I'd like to check out a concert with you. Why don't you ever invite me to one?"

He replied, "Are you sure you want to go? You don't seem like you're really into concerts. That one time you watched a football game, you were not very interested. It doesn't seem like music is all that important to you."

Amanda scratched her head because she went to a couple concerts while she was in Ireland and told him what a great time she had and even sent him pictures. And what did a football game have to do with concerts? Amanda stayed in her best self, "Well, I'd like to go to a concert with you and learn more about a band you like."

"Hmm, well I'll look into tickets. If I can find you a ticket, do you really want to go?" Amanda left the conversation feeling exhausted. The physical sensation was a little negative. She texted him a bit later and said that she was going to spend the day with her parents instead if he hadn't already bought tickets. Perhaps he didn't really want her along for his own reasons—he didn't want to spend the money or he wanted to enjoy one-on-one brother times. In any case, he got what he wished for. There are many possibilities. But she showed a sincere interest, and he resisted. She had information for the decision pile. Then she remembered back to that statement, "Women don't really mean what they say." And she was a woman.

She decided she didn't need to address it. She realized he also wasn't curious about what she liked or needed. That the kind of man she really wanted to be with would not need to overcome a huge hurdle of questioning what she said. That her ideal relationship partner would say, "I'd love for you to come. I hope you love them as much as I do." So, she could reply back, "I'm sure I will, and even if I don't, I just want to have that experience with you at least once so I'll know. We can't share all the same interests, but we won't know if we don't try a few together."

Just because you've begun to live more soulfully, don't suddenly force your new ways on your partner. That's called being a spiritual bully. Remember those religious zealots who found God and then forced it on some unsuspecting indigenous tribe because the missionaries were going to save them? Don't be that kind of spiritual warrior. Be the kind who lives in such light that you inspire those around you to be better. They will rise up to match you or reject you to feel better about themselves.

Chapter 10:

Elevate the Accountability Factor

The purpose of this chapter is to teach you how to elevate the accountability factor in your relationship and hold yourself and your partner accountable for your own outcomes. By this point in the book, you've probably noticed this is a guide focused on the process. And as you focus on executing the process, you'll continually get feedback. All this feedback is information for your decision pile that gives you your best outcome.

You have a clear vision for your best self so you can live and experience love every day. You know the qualities of your best self well enough to set powerful intentions that create a love bubble for you to function in. You know how to register the physical sensations in your body giving you information about what your essential self loves so you can maximize your one hundred units of energy.

You've been embracing your emotions and using them as powerful prompts. You've become more mindful and aware, noticing the difference between facts and fictions, being willing to try on new thoughts that create better outcomes. And you've been speaking up confidently, not a nag in sight. You've taken responsibility for yourself and the love you have in your life.

Sometimes, your partner will be onboard. Sometimes, they will not. Your job is not to make sure they do the same. Your job is to stay in your own business. The only thing you can control is yourself, so that is where you have the most power. If you put your energy into trying to change your partner, you will be focused on an outcome and they will feel coerced. All you can do is share your genuine feelings and make gentle and respectful requests. And see the information that comes back from that. Remember, it goes in the decision pile. If you are frustrated, ask yourself whose business am I in?

- Am I in my business?
- Am I in their business?
- Am I in God's business?

When someone crosses the line, you can calmly say, "That behavior is unacceptable." That's really the whole lesson.

Amanda and Ken were mid-trip in Ireland, on the way back from Belfast to Dublin. She had been to Belfast before, but it was new for Ken. He'd never been to Ireland. They were on a bus about to pick up a rental car in Dublin for a few days of countryside driving. They had been meal prepping the majority of their meals, eating almost the same things every day, and going on bus tours. They had been on a *Game of Thrones* bus tour and a Giant's Causeway bus tour. They had plans to go to the Guinness Storehouse in Dublin. Amanda had never watched *Game of Thrones* before the trip but caught up before Ken arrived so she could understand the references and try to enjoy the bus tours. She also didn't enjoy bus tours, but Ken was not keen on renting a car for the entire trip to save money. Amanda was fond of looking for hidden gem restaurants and learning about the local culture through the food. Ken hadn't done any restaurant research since he wasn't a foodie—food was just fuel. No one had done anything wrong, they just liked different things and were trying to merge different traveling styles. But Amanda wasn't feeling like it was much of a vacation. She wasn't enjoying herself. She needed to stop and ask whose business she was in.

- Is it my business to make sure I have a good time?
- Is it Ken's business?
- Is it God's business?

Amanda realized she needed something to really look forward to, so she booked dinner at a nice restaurant after the Guinness Storehouse tour. They had timed tickets for the tour and would be in the city center anyway. Amanda announced to Ken, "Dinner's on me." She wanted him to feel free to enjoy himself and thought it would be generous of her to treat him to something nicer than a pub. They ordered. Amanda asked a few questions and Ken gave one word answers. Amanda knew that part of what would make this enjoyable was chatting over a nice meal. In fact, Ken wasn't even looking at her.

Amanda asked, "What was your favorite part of the day?"

Ken replied, "Probably the Guinness Storehouse."

Then silence.

Amanda tried again, "What are you looking at?"

"Nothing much, outside."

Silence again.

Amanda looked around at the other tables, but there were only a handful of occupied tables. "I notice you looking over there. What do you see?"

"Oh, some people walking by."

Silence.

Finally, Amanda admitted to herself that this was not the kind of nice dinner date she had hoped for. It was probably the nicest restaurant they had ever been to, and he was taking all the fun out of it for her. She was starting to resent making the reservations. It hardly seemed worth it—she had paid to have a bad time with Ken. She stared at him at first just to see if he would look at her. He did, rather blankly, and then looked away. She made a final attempt at humor. She smiled and waved, "Hey, I'm over here!"

And Ken snapped. "You don't show any interest in what I have to say. You don't listen to me, and now suddenly I have to talk because you want to talk."

"Tell me more. When did I do that?"

"The entire trip."

"I'm sorry you felt that way. Why didn't you say anything sooner?"

"Because if it didn't go well, it would ruin the whole trip."

"Well, why don't you go ahead and get it out now? You can't really ruin dinner at this point. Can you give me a specific example of a time that you felt ignored?"

Ken looked miffed but tried to think of something. "Earlier today, I was telling you that story about how I was at a party with a Hollywood producer. Most people at that point would say something like, 'Tell me more,' or, 'Oh, that sounds interesting.' You didn't say anything."

"If it makes you feel better, I do remember that story. And I didn't say anything because I was listening. When I listen, I don't talk that much."

"Well, I think you're a bad listener."

"Perhaps different, but not bad. Listen, I did something that made you feel bad, and I'm happy to take responsibility for that. But the way you've been behaving at dinner? Your response is your responsibility. I welcome you pointing out when you don't feel heard. That's an open invitation. Next time it happens, feel free to say something when it happens so I can understand better what you're talking about.

Amanda continued. "I've been really looking forward to this dinner. It's the one thing on this trip that's really for me, and I'm pretty disappointed and hurt. I think it's passive-aggressive to not say anything about why you are upset and then punish me with the silent treatment. I've noticed you don't bring up your own issues separately. The past few times where I start to bring something to your attention, you've turned it around on me. You have a habit of hijacking my moments and it feels like defensive behavior. It's really not appropriate. I'd like you to find your own moments to address them. Otherwise, I feel like it's being petty. You only have something to say when I have something to say. I'd love to talk about how you feel after you've had some time to think about it."

Amanda was realizing and putting together how she felt as she talked. In the past when Ken got defensive, she let the conversation get side-swiped. Ken typically had a reason that would re-focus the blame onto Amanda. Like today, he had been stonewalling her at dinner, but it was her fault because she didn't say, "How interesting, tell me more" earlier and, according to him, for a number of other failures to listen well—but none that he could really articulate when asked to explain with specifics.

Amanda recognized that Ken's claims were probably based on real things and his real feelings. She didn't really fault him for not knowing exactly how to address them, that was human. But seeing how hard it was for him to accept responsibility and that his default seemed to be to deflect blame onto her was valuable information for the information pile. Did Amanda really want to be with someone who couldn't just say, "I'm sorry, I zoned out. Thanks for snapping me out of it"? Or, "Hey, I must be more sensitive than I realized. I got a bit upset earlier when I thought you were ignoring me. I didn't say anything but I guess it bothered me way more than I thought. Can we hit reset?"

Amanda observed the rule of threes. She had watched three previous conversations begin with her new nonviolent communication methods and each time it had been met with defensiveness. Ken seemed to find a reason each time that it was actually her fault—he was only behaving poorly in response to something she had done before.

She prepared herself for the next time, not knowing for sure that it would happen. And this time she realized it wasn't her business how Ken behaved, it was his. So she laid out the boundaries. Whether or not he finds his own moments to communicate when he feels hurt by Amanda is really his business. Amanda does not need to excuse his upbringing or his past. This is additional information for the decision pile. So she added these things to the pile: When Ken feels criticized, he gets defensive and turns the blame onto me. When Ken's feelings are hurt, he can be passive-aggressive. Instead of sharing how he feels, he makes his point by acting out.

What about Truly Unacceptable Behavior?

Anything that's remotely threatening to your safety and mental, emotional, or physical welfare is unacceptable. I've been fortunate that all my partners have been good to me. Not perfect, but genuine. I only had one boyfriend in all my years that I can say his true colors weren't pretty. His name was Gary. I had been in two back-to-back long-term monogamous relationships. One, I married. The other, I broke up with because I wasn't ready to get married and he was. Gary never wanted to get married or have kids. I was grateful to not have the pressure. But he was madly in love. I love to travel. To date I've been to over forty countries, and I'm easily prompted and inspired to travel. The holidays were nearing, and I was shooting the breeze.

I absentmindedly said, "I'd love to go to Thailand."

Gary responded, "If you go, don't bother coming back."

Alarm bells went off. Punishment doesn't fit the crime. He was basically threatening me. There had to be a story behind the story. I could threaten him back, but that really wasn't the best version of myself; I hardly wanted to stoop to his level. I decided to give him the benefit of the doubt, because that's what I do when I'm at my best.

"Hey, Gary, you can tell me that you don't want me to go. You can tell me that you were looking forward to spending the holidays together. You can tell me that you feel hurt or disappointed. But you can't threaten me. It's completely unacceptable behavior."

I paused to let it all sink in.

"Listen, I'm a traveler. I love it, and I'm easily inspired. I'm always going to say I want to go somewhere. Sometimes it'll happen, sometimes it won't. But I'm not going to stop sharing about it or talking about it. It's something I enjoy. Does that make sense?"

Gary's chin softened. He began slowly, "I've always hated the holidays. I was looking forward to finally having someone to spend the holidays with. And I was suddenly really disappointed imagining being alone again for the holidays."

Gary never threatened me again.

When something unacceptable happens, call it out. You don't need to escalate, scream, yell, and threaten. Just call it out immediately. Add the response to the information pile. Now you have all the tools you need to create a complete decision pile. You have all the information you need to ask yourself the most important questions.

Chapter 11:

A Perfect Day to Decide

This chapter is the culmination of your commitment to the process—a perfect day will happen that will allow you to determine the best path forward. You will experience a best day for your relationship. This is how your relationship will look under the best conditions—not perfect conditions, but the best real-world conditions.

All the tools in the prior chapters will help you get to this day because you have been moving through the process. It's not actually a day on the calendar you mark and say, "That's going to be the best day for our relationship." It will happen, and then you will know. You will have implemented everything in this book, and your decision pile will be complete. You can add little bits to it, but nothing will fundamentally change; the main meal is all there. Here's what it looked like for Mike and Lucy.

They had run into each other a few times over the years but were in other relationships. But then they both happened to be single and crossed paths in Cuba, of all places. Lucy wasn't sure Mike was relationship material, but he began to pursue her. Slowly at first, but once the pace picked up, they spent almost every day together.

The things that bothered Lucy most were the age difference and their relationship goals. But they had such a good time together, so she kept collecting information. By the time she came to me they had been to Europe together. The trip was wonderful. And then it hit her: this was their best day. This would be the best their relationship would ever be. He didn't really want to get married again, and she still did. So a few fun trips was all he could really offer her, not building a life together. She imagined having all the love that she could possibly want or need. And it filled her with so much confidence that she decided to end things. More time together would bond them more, but it wouldn't change that they wanted different things out of it. Lucy still wanted to be in love, and she realized that it would be hard to fall in love knowing that there was a fixed end. She realized that if she had all the love she wanted and needed, she would never just accept a few trips in exchange for a shot at a partnership. This was a perfect day to decide. She was ready to leave.

Ken and Amanda

Amanda felt like she'd never been more flexible and accommodating of someone with such a fixed and regimented life. Ken didn't accommodate her much, but she felt better living up to her best self. After their trip to Ireland, instead of focusing on what she liked and didn't like, the pros and cons list, she examined her overall energy. She tapped into the wisdom of her body and her essential self. When he left, she breathed a sigh of relief. I asked her if the energy felt expansive, contracting or if there was no change. She thought it was fairly flat. If she was being honest, just a bit on the negative side, like a minus one. That's pretty good information for the decision pile. It was her first vacation with someone that felt a bit like work with a relatively low payoff. Back home they had a great sex life, but they only saw each other once a week. They had sex every day on the trip, but it was never quite as good as back home. More information for the decision pile.

When I asked what her heart was telling her, she remembered that day she had rolled up into a ball and cried like a banshee after finding out he was doing a cleanse with his brother over the holidays. More information for the decision pile.

Amanda constantly asked herself if her thoughts were true when she thought he was being stingy or cheap. She came up with the more neutral thought that being frugal with his money has allowed him to pursue a creative career.

A few days after the trip, Ken emailed an itemized expense list for Ireland and asked what her expenses were. When she saw the list, she started feeling petty. Ken ate two to three times more but he wanted to split the costs. Amanda had also purchased food items before his arrival and never kept track. She actually thought the planning and meal prep labor she took on saved him money. It was a "for us" move. She had paid for bus tickets, castle entries and a number of things that she didn't think to keep track of. She didn't need to go to Belfast again, but he was a big Game of Thrones fan. In fact, they could have stayed in Dublin for free, but he wanted to see other parts of Ireland like Cliffs of Moher, where she'd already been. It was a trip focused on his priorities, save one dinner that was for her that ended up being not that enjoyable. She realized that being petty was not her best self. She would have to reframe the conversation the next time she talked to Ken.

Amanda said, "I noticed you sent me an itemized expense list. Why did you send that? I've never received one of these before."

Ken replied, 'I thought we were going to split the costs."

"If you wanted to share costs, in my experience, you could share up front your budget and then you could ask me mine. And then we could decide how to prioritize. I had a place for us to stay in Dublin; we didn't need to do all those things, but you wanted to. In fact, I've been to Belfast and Cliffs of Moher before. Despite that, I considered what was the most generous I could be so I paid for the hotel in Belfast. It was the single most expensive line item of the entire trip. And the most expensive meal was also the one I paid for."

She realized he had a money story rooted in scarcity: there was never enough and it had nothing to do with her. Even though she managed not to take it personally, her physical sensation score was sending her signals. And even if she didn't have the exact correct assessment, that wouldn't change the way it affected her energy. She was anxious every time she interacted with him and money was involved. Her essential self did not like it and that was never going away. This went into the decision pile.

She had practiced all the transformational conversation techniques and she noted he was prone to being defensive and passive-aggressive. Not always, but it took vast amounts of her one hundred available units of energy to discuss relatively small things. They hadn't even hit a major problem together. She added that information to the decision pile.

Amanda had finally gotten to put the accountability into practice. She was responsible for her response; he was responsible for his. When they got back from Ireland, Ken was making more of an effort for date nights. He got tickets for them to go see *When Harry Met Sally*. He made a plan. The execution was a bit rough; he wasn't in good form at the start, forgetting to open her doors, but she felt with all the information she had that this was the best he could do. He was doing his best. It had happened. This was their version of a best day.

I asked, "If he never changes, could you live with it?"

Amanda said, "No."

"If this is the best that it'll ever be, could you live with it?"

"No."

They had a great sex life, and he was a nice guy, but mentally and emotionally, there was very little holding them together. And their future would be a disaster. She also had a few extra pieces of information prior to that. She had a pool day with her friend Donna when Ken attended a concert with Cory. A matchmaker approached them and asked if they were single. They both raised their hands and said, "Yes we are."

Amanda noted later that she was not mad at Ken or trying to get back at him; it was her honest immediate unfiltered reaction. Information noted. That same week she was meeting a friend for dinner across town. She passed Ken's home on the way over. Later Amanda recalled the experience as unusual. In her other relationships, she would normally reach out to her boyfriend to see if their schedules might sync up for a drop-in. All her other relationships had a lot more daily contact and connection. Ken's bandwidth was about once or twice a week. She had been open to trying something new with a bit more freedom, but it left her feeling unattached. Information for the decision pile.

I asked, "So, if we ask your future self if this is really the person by your side, what does she say?"

Amanda said, "No."

It had become so clear to Amanda that she could not wait to break up with Ken. They already had their best day;

no better days were coming. And she had so much information in the decision pile.

She asked to see him that night.

Amanda started, "I really care about you. I have loving feelings in my heart for you, but I feel like it's time to end our time together."

Because she'd been showing up confidently and speaking up, he was not caught off guard. While he didn't expect a breakup that day, it wasn't completely out of the blue. All the issues were on the table. Amanda held his face and kissed his forehead. "Thank you for doing your best. I know you tried. I did my best, too, and I'll miss you."

They clung to each other one last time.

Ken said, "This is the most mutual and nicest breakup I've ever had."

Amanda replied, "I know. I'm glad."

It was harder with me and Ben. These are all the tools I wish I'd had. My regrets with him were that I had no way to share how I was feeling. And while I felt the truth of my essential self speaking to me, I didn't know how to trust it. I wrote this book so no one would ever have to suffer that much for making the right decision. The longer I stayed, the more painful it became to unravel. But it took so much of my hundred units of energy to stay that I felt like I was cheating myself. My essential self wanted to go on a great adventure and experience life in a way that I could not with Ben.

So, what do I tell people? I tell people that Ben and I were young. He was my first boyfriend and I was his first girlfriend. We were each other's first real relationship. We were both virgins until our wedding day. Some people marry young and get lucky. Some people wait until they're married to have sex and get lucky. Despite being a great match on paper and checking off all the boxes, we didn't have much natural chemistry for one another. This is a true explanation in a way that most can understand.

But exchange chemistry for energy. Because of our mental and physical resources, we tried. We applied the things we learned in therapy and counseling, but the big looming problem was my essential self and his essential self were a mismatch. We had a friendship sure, but as life-long lovers and mates, together we weren't a good fit. In the end, we did stop having sex. Days became weeks became months became years. The body is a physical container of energy and mine was telling me that something was amiss. I tell people we don't know what we don't know. I wrote this book so you can know. So your decision pile will have all the information you need. When your best day comes to pass, you'll not only know, you'll have a clear and loving path forward.

Your information pile will have at its foundation the sensations and ratings you got from visualizing a future together and a future apart. You'll have the responses you received from leading with love. You'll see the results from reframing your thoughts. Added to that will be the impact of being able to have conversations that matter and elevating the accountability factor. When the best day comes, you'll know it. You'll be ready to see everything with clarity. More importantly, you'll be at peace with yourself. Now that you've been living by your best qualities, you'll feel more connected to your soul. This is the way you've imagined yourself to be. To be able to live like that is a gift that no one can take from you. Plus it will give you the confidence to make hard choices. To live bravely, authentically, honorably—that is love.

Chapter 12:

No Regrets

You've been thinking about this for years, trying to make a decision about whether you stay or leave. It's time for a no-regrets decision. You're in the relationship, but you're not all there. And now you've waited so long you're not sure how to move forward. But you want to. You don't want to have this regret hanging over you for years. You can't imagine living this way any longer. You're committed to finally figuring it out once and for all.

And guess what? You deserve to live in love with your head held high. You can look yourself in the mirror and go to bed every night with the confidence of knowing you made the right choice. It's completely possible. But here are some challenges that might stop you and keep you in the stay-or-go cycle.

The Old Pros and Cons List

The old pros and cons list will be the number-one reason keeping you in the vicious indecision cycle. Since most everyone around you thinks in these terms, it'll be hard to break out of that.

You might actually have to cut off some friends and family while you decide. They are speaking to your social self obligations. Most of what they say will not be for your benefit but for their own. It's not their fault. It's a reflection of what matters to them; they don't understand the concept of fostering your essential self. You'll immediately find yourself falling into the old habit of pros and cons.

Sometimes it'll be in defense of staying. Sometimes it'll be in defense of leaving. Either way, you'll be on the defense because that's what happens when you invite others into your business. Amanda had to stop sharing her thoughts about Ken with her friends. She realized they all had their own struggles and insecurities and what they said to her reflected more about what was happening for them than her.

This book gives you the tools for you to stay in your own business, but you're the only one who has read it.

Fear

Another major challenge is fear. Your social self has many fears. Fear of your partner's feelings, your parents' expectations, and your children's perceptions. So, let's say all together, that is six people. We think the whole world cares so much about this decision. There are about seven billion people who do not care what you decide. But fear is a powerful motivator. And it'll reinforce your habit of making fear-based decisions instead of love-based decisions—not exactly a formula for a happy and dynamic life filled with love and freedom.

Change Is Hard

It'll be hard to break your own habits and thought patterns. You already know this, because if that weren't the case, you would have already decided. But changing does not require years of therapy and counseling. Those can be helpful in supporting your mental health, but that won't necessarily mean you make meaningful progress in deciding what is best for you and your relationship.

Comfort

Then there's the comfort factor. The first part of that is sunk costs. You already put so much in; you'll count that as a reason to stay. The second part is making room for uneasy emotions since part of the process is allowing yourself to feel your feelings. If you've never done that before, you'll find reasons to escape. You'll start to notice your feelings and end up flipping on the TV for a Netflix binge.

Accountability

This process takes commitment. And if you haven't been living a life where you take accountability for how you've been showing up, it'll be challenging. Without a coach to keep you accountable, how will you guarantee that you will follow through?

Encouragement

One major challenge to implementing this process is the lack of support and encouragement. Those first transformational conversations probably won't be great, because you're practicing in real time with another human being who hasn't signed on to have transformational conversations. You'll have to dust yourself off and try again.

Amanda knew her early conversations with Ken fell flat. She learned she needed to get better at the compliment sandwich. She tried giving feedback by starting off with a positive acknowledgment first, and the next round got better. You'll want some support as you go through this. I suggested that Amanda only share with her friends who could just hold space for her but didn't feel the need to give her advice.

You'll have to look around and ask yourself if any of your friends are capable of holding space, witnessing and acknowledging what you are feeling, express their support and care, and then not give you well-meaning advice.

It sounds like this: "I have some things I want to share with you, but since I'm still in the middle of my decision, can you listen without judgment? This is a new process I'm trying. I think listening without judgment would sound something like this for me: 'Thank you for sharing.

That sounds difficult. I'm sorry you are going through that. I wish I could make it better. I am here for you and I love you.'"

You'll determine the exact words in the Ring of Fire exercise. When you emerge, you can say to yourself what you hope to hear and then you can share that with one or two of your closest friends that you can trust to stay in their own business. If you don't have any, this process can be a lonely road.

Trust

Another major challenge is trusting yourself as you navigate a new process you have never tried before. Your essential self is not going to steer you in the wrong direction. You have every safeguard in place with this process.

Conclusion:

Clear Me, Clear Heart, Clear Path Forward

I remember how hard it was to leave my marriage and how long it took. Because I wasn't confident in my decision, I missed opportunities to make the process of leaving easier on both of us. When I discovered coaching, I wished I had all those tools. I wrote this book so no one would have to suffer in limbo or to spend thousands of dollars on therapy and barely make a dent in the decision process. I can't believe I missed the most important things that were right under my nose the entire time. So, I took all the tools and refined the process to create a clear and loving path forward. You deserve to live in love every day of your life!

"Should I Leave My Relationship or Not?"

That's the question that's been hanging over you. It's what led you to reading this book and committing to the process. You wanted a clear and loving path forward.

- You wanted to make a decision free from fear and guilt.
- You wanted to stop torturing yourself with doubt and uncertainty.
- You wanted to lift the emotional burden you felt saddled with.
- Ultimately, you wanted to be confident that you had all the information necessary to face yourself and your loved ones and move forward.

In Chapter 4, you were able to get super clear on the top qualities of your best self. This is who you are when you have all the love you could want and need. Ultimately, becoming this person is what allows you to attract the love you want and need. You become this person for yourself first and foremost. When you are in this space, there's no room for fear and guilt, only love and the qualities of your best self will consume you.

In Chapter 5, you learned how to set a powerful intention for your interactions, in essence creating a love bubble. You learned this is the quality that you bring to a situation. It's the way you are showing up in the world for yourself and your relationship. It allows your partner to interact with a more authentic version of you.

In Chapter 6, you learned to trust in the wisdom of

your body. You learned how to connect with your essential self. You tapped into this truth that is all your own by scanning your body for physical sensations. You learned to name these sensations and give them a number score. This is the foundation of your decision pile. This gave you the ability to stop overthinking, spending all your energy on what your social self is consumed by. You are now able to comprehend what it means to have one hundred units of energy, this special combination of your mental, emotional and physical resources. Your new understanding of how different people and situations will support or take away those resources gives you the vital information you need to stop the doubt and uncertainty.

In Chapter 7, you unlocked the strength in your heart. You embraced the emotional maturity necessary to face your emotions fully—to experience this beautiful condition of the human existence and choose acceptance of yourself. You now have the power to ask in a curious and playful way what information your heart is sharing with you about your deepest needs and desires. If you don't ask, the answer is always no. Now you have the power to ask the universe for the desires of your heart. You also get to see what becomes of your kind requests and add that information to the information pile.

In Chapter 8, you learned to examine the thoughts in your mind. There are circumstances and then there are the thoughts you think about those circumstances that generate feelings, which creates results. You can reframe your beliefs to generate new outcomes. You can let go of the judgments about your partner and yourself that have kept you stuck in indecision.

In Chapter 9, you learned how to share and talk about the process you've been going through—to show up confidently and speak up. You can be a source of inspiration and self-discovery for your partner. Your changes can also be a source of painful self-reflection. They've been watching you and responding. These are conversations that will continue to transform the relationship. This has given you insightful information about the nature of your relationship and how you interact with one another.

In Chapter 10, you stepped into authentic accountability. These are boundaries that hold everyone involved responsible for how they respond. You'll know how to stay in your business and release all responsibility for changing your partner. This will empower you to be the best version of yourself, because it says that you trust your partner to grow and mature in their own time at their own pace. Demanding anything more is as punishing to them as your negative self-talk and social self-pressure has been to you.

In Chapter 11, you got to see the culmination of your commitment to love and your essential self, the way you honored the relationship and the essential self of the other person. You'll be resolute in your "knowing," because you've done all the work. With all the information in your decision pile, you'll have your decision about whether you should leave or not, and have a clear path forward.

My wish for you is that you'll read this book, find the relief you've been hoping for, and see that the answer is love. You can be your kind and loving self and still make a big "scary" decision. I wanted to shine grace and compassion on you as you navigate a new path forward. Where you show up every day as the grown-up woman the little girl in you always wanted to be. Welcome to this transformation into your best self, where you have all the love you want and need.

Acknowledgments

I believe in open communication, saying I love you, fighting for what matters, and journeys over destinations. I'd like to acknowledge some of the people who helped me live up to what I believe in so that I could write and publish this book.

To Alison Singh Gee, my instructor at the UCLA Extension Writers' Program six years ago—thank you for fanning the spark that there was indeed a story in me that needed to be written. You took our dedicated little group and pushed us to create beautiful, raw, and transportive work. To my classmates, thank you for keeping me mesmerized and spellbound by your words. The talent in that room was astounding. It was my privilege to be a part of that magic.

To my first book coach Alexa Bigwarfe—I marvel at your passion for books and the women who write them.

When you mentioned that my book publication date was the eighth anniversary of your daughter's death—the whole reason you started this journey—my heart gasped. Kat Biggie, your time on earth was so brief, only two days, but the impact you made was huge and lives on.

To my next book coach, Sarah Saint-Laurent—you're a force of nature and agent of change in a world that desperately needs feminine strength and positive transformation. Thank you for guiding our Writer's Circle with your expertise and inspired support. You use your gifts and ability to see around the bend in such remarkable fashion, inspired.

To Angela Lauria and The Author Incubator team, you're the village helping me cross the publishing finish line. To my developmental editor, Ora North, and managing editor, Emily Tuttle—thanks for your patience and encouragement. Many more thanks to everyone else at TAI, but especially Ramses Rodriguez and Cheyenne Giesecke for always keeping things moving forward. Thank you for taking my wide-eyed wonder and turning it into a living, breathing, published book.

Thank you to David Hancock and the Morgan James Publishing team for helping me bring this book to print.

To Bonnie Koo, our paths have crossed in such remarkable ways. I am so grateful to have shared heart-to-hearts, delicious meals, house swaps, coaching tips, business advice, and so much more. Hoping to hunt croissants in Paris and agnolotti del plan in Piedmont again. While it's incredible that you have also become a fellow author, coach and business maven, what I love most is that you've been a trusted friend through it all.

To my beloved coaching colleagues, you make the world a better place. Jennifer Winfield, Marti Keefer, Gloria Mosher Walker, Chere Clark, Nona Jordan, Patty Manning Lennon, Heather Vickery, Steph Lagana. All of you have helped me hold my head higher. As true leaders, you show up and give first before you ask others to follow. And a special shout out to Heather LeRoss for being the first author in our little coaching group—see what you started!

To JT Aupetit, you're a beautiful human being and your kindness has been a treasure. I'm so grateful to you for sharing your love of nature with me and keeping me close to mother earth. One of these days, we will actually make our great travel abroad tour happen! Thank you for believing in me, supporting me and getting your whole family to support my book launch.

To my friends—of which there are too many to mention, but I will name the ones I have spoken to during the writing of this book—thank you for making me feel lucky: Quyenzi Dang Pham, Jean Rhee, Marilyn Hsiung, Simran Kaleka, Divya Shokeen Khalsa, Sonia Kalaria, Tarla Makaeff, Tinger Hseih, Bella Graham, Rashi Khanna Wiese, and Audrey Lo. How is it possible to have so many smart, beautiful and talented people who care about me enough to take my calls and check up on me?!? Love you all!

To all the wonderful souls I have encountered in my travels, I did my best to take every positive experience and take it back home with me until one day I realized that no matter where I went, I was home. The stories and experiences became part of the fabric of my everyday life. No matter where I go, I can wander with wonder. When I first started traveling, I delighted in the kindness of strangers. After many years, I now realize these are just friends waiting to meet me.

Which leads me to Bali, Indonesia. This magical place has its own life-force. I spent a month solo here in November eight years ago recovering from a broken leg, and it nurtured my body, mind and soul. From that time, I knew that it was my purpose to give others courage when they needed it most. I have come full circle and am making good on that promise as a coach and author. And I have returned to you, Bali, to pay homage and to live in awe and gratitude as I launch the Kindle version of this book.

And then there's Vietnam. Spending my days here in Ho Chi Minh putting the finishing touches on the print version of my book is truly a dream come true. I have been so happy and grateful, my heart wants to explode. Being able to live what I preach about designing a life that gives full expression to my essential self is magical. The energy and rush this place gives me has been a treasure.

To Ann Tran, your love and friendship is without bounds. You've been a part of every big and scary decision I've made in the past five years. Thank you for doing life with me. Grateful is really an understatement with you.

To my dad, I love you for supporting me even though you don't understand what I do or why I do it. When I graduated from high school, you gave me some sage advice. "There are some great things about the Taiwanese way. There are some great things about the American way. Neither one is perfect. You can take the best of both." Thank you for telling me in heartfelt-dad fashion to find my own way.

To my nephew Connor, you make my heart sing. Thank you for making me laugh and play with you every day when I visit. You give me so much joy and presence. It's what I want to inspire in my readers.

I believe it's the people that put the "good" in the good life! Thank you dear friends, loved ones, and treasured readers for making my life more than good—it's exquisite.

Thank You

I know that you called out to the universe for clarity, and it conspired on your behalf to give you what you need. This book landed in your hands to give you a clear and loving path forward for your relationship. I want to support you in that as much as possible.

Send your email to live@thelinlife.com for a free video to guide you through a body scan of the physical sensations in your body. Learn this foundational technique as you begin your decision-making process with confidence and ease.

I would love to learn more about your journey and success in pursuing the relationship of your dreams. Please keep in touch on Instagram (https://www.instagram.com/thelinlifellc/) and share your wins. I'm so grateful for the energy you have devoted to reading this book. I hold that energy as sacred and am sending you so much love right now!

About the Author

Karen Lin is an engineer turned life coach who helps women in STEM become leaders in their industry. She worked on the design, construction, and project management of many multimillion-dollar infrastructure projects before turning her attention to engineering new outcomes for people's lives.

Karen became a life coach after her coach training with the Martha Beck Institute (MBI). She was inspired to write the book *Should I Leave My Relationship or Not* by her clients. They were smart, confident and successful in their careers but felt uncertain in how to proceed in their personal and romantic relationships. Karen developed a process for her clients to have a clear path forward. Through her one-on-one coaching, she works with her clients to gain clarity and peace.

Karen has lost her Texan twang but not her oversized heart. Born in Taipei, she was three when her family immigrated to Texas. She attended the engineering college at the University of Texas at Austin, where she obtained her degree in civil engineering. Raised in a Taiwanese home that valued education, family, and hard work, she continues to be a lifelong learner and supports women as leaders in STEM.

Karen currently lives in Los Angeles, California, and loves food, travel, art—anything that engages her to be actively present. She looks back on each heartache and disappointment she has experienced with gratitude for what it has taught her about the importance of having a constant source of love and joy in each person's life. She believes every woman deserves to have as much confidence and success in her relationships as she does in her career.

Website: https://thelinlife.com

Email: Live@thelinlife.com

Facebook: https://www.facebook.com/thelinlife

9 781631 951169